# NAMING  THE  IDOLS

*To Latin American friends and colleagues
who have helped me to envision
a new future for my country*

# NAMING THE IDOLS

### Biblical Alternatives for U.S. Foreign Policy

*Richard Shaull*

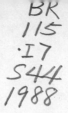

ME Y ER
STONE
BOOKS

Published in the United States by Meyer-Stone Books,
a division of Meyer, Stone, and Company, Inc.,
714 South Humphrey, Oak Park, IL 60304

Cover design: Terry Dugan Design

Manufactured in the United States of America
92 91 90 89 88          5 4 3 2 1

---

**Library of Congress Cataloging in Publication Data**

Shaull, Richard.
    Naming the idols.

    1. Christianity and international affairs.
2. United States — Foreign relations — 1981-
I. Title.
BR115.I7S44    1988          261.8'7          87-62872
ISBN 0-940989-32-8

# CONTENTS

# FOREWORD

*by Richard Falk*

After reading this book, I would rather entrust the foreign policy of this country to Richard Shaull than to our present State Department, no matter which party is in the White House and regardless of who is selected to serve as Secretary of State.

This preference of mine expresses both what is wrong with mainstream foreign policy and what is persuasive about Shaull's alternative vision. The American mainstream, that is, embracing both political parties, the government bureaucracy, the influential media, and the leading academic pundits, has endorsed the view that the cold war framework should indefinitely guide our involvement in the Third World, especially enabling a clear line to be drawn between friends and enemies, between what is desirable and what is unacceptable. Of course, there are recurrent tactical disputes. The main instance of the moment is whether or not it is worth helping the contras, with the issue being posed almost entirely in relation to their prospects. There is no mainstream disposition to support the Sandinistas as the best government in the region or to acknowledge it as already the most successful in Nicaragua's sorrowful history. There is instead a near unanimous condemnation by the mainstream of the Sandinistas that seems frozen by a stereotype of evil that hides behind the label "Marxist-Leninist." Such an outlook, especially to the extent it validates covert operations, and even private diplomacy of the sort revealed by the Iran/contra disclosures, pushes this country into alignment with some of the most murderous and destructive forces at large in the world, it places us on the losing side of history, and associates patriotism with mindless anti-Communism.

Such a stance, *in extremis,* accounts for the readiness of our policy-makers to wage nuclear war, even to devote billions to the development of first-strike weapons systems and so-called defensive technologies. Since we associate our side with the good and theirs with evil, whatever makes us stronger seems justifiable even if it risks human survival itself, and even if it puts future generations beneath a darkening cloud. Periodic arms control agreements and superpower summits, although welcome, can do little to arrest this basic momentum or challenge the apocalyptic mind-set of the nuclearists who control our underlying attitude toward national security.

Against such a heavy burden no marginal effort to change things is worth much. The underlying worldview that leads us to associate our national interests with reactionary forces of order and oppression is essentially beyond the framework of national debate. In this year of presidential elections it is a virtual certainty that no serious candidate will question mainstream assumptions, and if he (or she) does, that candidate's prospects of success would be immediately diminished by carefully coordinated media attacks on "credibility," suitably disguised as raising doubts about whether the particular individual has the understanding or the toughness to uphold U.S. national interests in a hostile world.

In effect, at this time we cannot realistically look either to our political leadership or our electoral process to debate the sort of fundamental issues that need to be addressed if we are to find the strength and wisdom to escape from the vicious dead-end character of our foreign policy. It is for these reasons that *Naming the Idols* is such a valuable and exhilarating book. Both its language and outlook manage a clean break with the foreign policy mainstream. Shaull relies on an entirely different framework to assess what it is we should, as a country, be seeking overseas and tests and confirms that framework by years of direct experience with the peoples and situations discussed. The focus is on the United States relationship to the Third World, most particularly Central America. It is a kind of gospel, bearing tidings of good news, that the oppressed peoples of the region are organizing their own liberation on the basis of a vision that peace and justice are attainable goals and that control of a nation's resources and government by a tiny privileged, often corrupt, elite serving foreign interests is unacceptable, unbearably so.

The most exciting feature of Shaull's testimony is its double validation. He explores with great lucidity the biblical basis for action in history, and interprets the Judeo-Christian imperative as requiring a believer to address the plight of the poor and oppressed as a primary spiritual concern. And he reinforces this normative outlook with the claim that Third World revolutionary politics in this hemisphere is increasingly inspired by precisely this vision, which has been gradually transforming the role of churches and the impact of religion. He is especially impressed by the emergence of Christian base communities and by the practice of the Sandinistas as the first political movement that bears the imprint of this new religious involvement in the struggles of the oppressed.

In the course of such explorations *Naming the Idols* considers both the challenge and possibilities of collaboration with Marxism and Marxists. Shaull acknowledges that the Marxist outlook is fundamentally opposed to oppressive forms of economic, political, and cultural domination in the region, and, further, that Marxists in the Third World are themselves most often ardent nationalists who are as suspicious of Moscow as Washington, and who have come over the years to appreciate their own affinity with the biblical perspective construed non-dogmatically, deepening their own mandate for struggle against injustice and bringing to bear language and symbolism that are trusted by the masses. Shaull is aptly fascinated by the Sandinista experience in Nicaragua because it seems to have evolved out of a fruitful cross-fertilizing process between Marxists and Christians. As well, it clarifies the position of the old church and the United States as united in their resolve to crush such movements of liberation.

Of course, it is depressing to realize that the United States has mobilized its military might for a sustained assault on Nicaragua's political experiment, and that no principled opposition to this assault has been managed by either the Democratic Party or by those who profess liberalism as their political creed. This sustained military pressure by a superpower on a small, poor, beleaguered country like Nicaragua produces great suffering, but even more troubling in the longer run, it spoils the experiment and may even lead to its collapse. A fledgling Sandinista government has had to concentrate its meager resources and energies upon the priorities of national defense, creating an initially unwanted prominence for military personnel and a permanent sense of emergency. Such tendencies work against democratization, especially when many of the forces of dissent are financed from the same sources as the mercenary troops that comprise the contras and are staffed by the remnants of Somoza's National Guard.

This Nicaraguan case, even granting its complexity and elusiveness, contains within it the whole process of action and reaction that lies at the center of Shaull's argument and vision. It is not enough to stop supporting the contras; we must find the moral and spiritual understanding of the aspirations of the Nicaraguan people and, to meet the hardest challenge of all, to apply that understanding here in the United States as well. If I have read *Naming the Idols* correctly, Shaull is convinced that we Americans cannot be true to our biblical heritage or to our own hallowed revolutionary past unless we renounce the idols — of wealth and of the demonized other, the enemy.

Shaull reaches this understanding, as I have suggested, by biblical study and through direct experience. There are other ways, as well. He acknowledges as much by his sensitive treatment of Marxism. But there are additional paths up the mountain. The fine Indian jurist Upendra Baxi has depicted such a comparable vision in his writings, reclaiming law and politics for the peoples of India by taking suffering seriously. The late Roy Preiswerk of Switzerland, influenced by his experience in the Caribbean, including marriage to a Grenadan, devoted his most mature academic work to dealing with international relations as if human beings mattered. There are strong grassroots tendencies evident in Buddhist and Hindu circles throughout Asia that parallel the sort of approach to religion and politics that Richard Shaull derives from the Bible. The global scope of this visionary reawakening to the central meaning of life being associated with our individual and collective responses to suffering is a source of hope and cross-cultural enrichment. We all by now realize that the dynamics of the world are increasingly integrated, whether it be the collapse of financial markets or currencies, the erosion of the ozone layer, the challenge of famine and disease in sub-Saharan Africa, or the struggle against the extremes of racism in South Africa.

Cultural diversity is one of the most valuable resources of this planet. To protect ourselves against any implication of ideological imperialism, it is important to admit, I believe, that the biblical message is not exclusive, and that other ways to obtain a comparable understanding are being effectively developed by non-Western spiritual traditions, and that we can learn much from contact with these developments. At the same time, for most of us in the West this message is transmitted most coherently and profoundly through our principal sacred text, the Bible, and it is generally by exploring our own spiritual roots that we create the best prospect for a broad shift in cultural mood of the sort that will be required if we are to carry the message of Shaull's book into the world.

The emphasis on the Bible, as sacred text, is very central to Richard Shaull's particular rendering of the message. I think others with an equivalent receptivity to the same vision might find their inspiration more through the life of Jesus or by reference to the teaching of a particular thinker (say, Thomas Merton) than by a concentration on the Bible. I have worked some with the Ground Zero group of nuclear resisters in the Seattle region of Washington, and I have been struck by their ecumenical religious orientation that seems as receptive to Gandhi as to Jesus and that seeks its vindication in action by rigid adherence to patterns of unconditional non-violence and love. These observations are not meant as criticism of Shaull's way of proceeding. On the contrary. It would dilute the power and depth of *Naming the Idols* if Shaull were to temper his scriptural mind-set by a more eclectic approach. I benefitted, especially, from his close and perceptive readings of Exodus, the Prophets, and the Book of Revelation.

We are left with a vision, a direction for politics, and an account of their embodiment in many parts of Latin America. But what of the United States? Shaull comments favorably on the Sanctuary Movement and on such religiously based initiatives as the programs of Witness for Peace. He sees these developments as responsive to and complementary with the positive tendencies that he finds in the Third World. And yet one feels that in the United States such expressions of discontent remain marginal, even in the religious domain. Unlike the Third World, suffering here at home has not yet catalyzed a widespread grassroots movement that acknowledges the central need to revitalize democracy and to alter the whole notion of how the United States should relate to the rest of the world. Such a movement may be waiting to be born, and *Naming the Idols* might, in retrospect, be appreciated as part of the birthing process.

It would be misleading to claim that the overall religious mood in the United States is currently very encouraging these days. There has been in recent years an unprecedented rise of fundamentalism and evangelical Christianity, with its stress on personal salvation and its literalist submission of the spirit to the secular forces to state power. In the name of freedom and democracy, such religious renderings prepare us all for "the rapture" of nuclear war and its place in working out God's supposedly bloody conception of the beginning and ending of human history. Such fundamentalism is itself a sign that the old order is breaking down, representing a kind of desperate last gasp, but it reminds us that religion, including the Bible, can serve idols as well as the cause of spiritual awakening. Of course, *Naming the Idols* is sensitive to this danger, although it never connects it very directly with the thought and practice of religion in the United States.

My hope is that as many people as possible, from many backgrounds, will read and discuss Richard Shaull's book. It offers us much wisdom with great clarity, and it invites an array of reinterpretations and extensions to the varied circumstances of struggle against oppression. I hope, too, that it will be a signal of an American awakening, issuing a call for a new patriotism that is at last attentive to what is at once ennobling in our history and promising in our destiny.

RICHARD FALK

# PREFACE

THIS BOOK IS THE PRODUCT of a personal struggle that began
forty-five years ago, when I went to live and work in Colombia,
Latin America, as a Presbyterian missionary and came face to face
with the human suffering caused by poverty. I was confronted daily
by the fact that vast numbers of men, women, and children were
deprived of everything I took for granted as absolutely essential
for human existence: enough food to eat, a decent place to live,
regular work, and access to medical care as well as educational
opportunities for their children. Gradually I came to realize that
this poverty was not something they had brought upon themselves
but rather the result of unjust economic and political structures
that served the interests of a very small elite rather than those of
the people; structures of exploitation produced by human greed,
but also structures that could be changed.

Living in that situation as a North American citizen and a
committed Christian turned out to be profoundly disturbing. For
I soon discovered that my country was very much involved in creating this order of privilege for the few and poverty for the many and
that it maintained close ties with those who most profited from it
and helped them stay in power. My religious faith, on the other
hand, had sensitized my conscience to the suffering of the poor
and led me to stand with them in their struggle for a better life.
It compelled me to pay attention not only to what was happening
economically and politically in Latin America but also to what the
United States was doing in that part of the world.

In 1952, I was transferred to Brazil and began working in close
association with Student Christian Movement throughout Latin
America. These involvements provided me with an unusual opportunity to broaden and deepen my understanding of the social

problems of the continent as well as U.S. policy in the region. I became more aware of the growing aspirations of dispossessed peoples, of the emerging popular movements seeking major changes in society, and of pressures building up across the continent for national self-determination, economically and politically. I realized that all these developments had profound implications for U.S. policy, yet I saw little evidence that our policymakers were taking them into account. The intervention of the CIA in Guatemala in 1954 to overthrow the first democratically elected government in that country working for moderate social reforms convinced me that my government was moving in a direction that would lead to more interventions and alienate us from the progressive democratic forces across the continent. As my work with the World Student Christian Federation gave me an opportunity to travel in Asia and Africa and meet many student leaders from Third World countries, I came to the conclusion that the struggles taking place in Latin America had many parallels in other parts of the world, and that the issue of North-South relations would take on increasing importance for the United States in the years ahead.

During these same years, I was privileged to be part of a unique group of Protestants and Catholics in Latin America who came together to study social and political issues from a faith perspective, a group made up of theologians and economists, politicians and political scientists, leaders of student and labor movements. These studies helped me to see much more clearly the urgent need for systemic change in Latin America as well as what the U.S.A. was doing to block this type of change. At the same time, our theological studies were providing us with new insight into what the Bible has to say about social justice, about the God who is "making all things new" and the calling of Christians to express love by working for a radical transformation of the world.

With this background, it's hardly surprising that recent developments in Central America and in U.S. policy in that region should not only gain my attention but compel me to become more involved. In 1984, my wife and I decided to free ourselves from work responsibilities here in order to spend six months living and working in Nicaragua, hoping in this way to get to know firsthand what was happening there. Since that time I have made several trips to the region and have spent a great deal of time studying the situation there. As a result, I find that the deeper my understanding of developments taking place, the greater my uneasiness about U.S. policy. My contacts with the people in urban and rural areas, the majority of whom are poor, and with pastoral agents sharing their struggles, have made me aware of the vitality and depth of their religious faith, their commitment to liberation struggles, and the fact that they are often targeted for death by those in power in El Salvador and Guatemala, or by the contras in Nicaragua. And as I have studied the Bible with them, something else has occurred. As I have been confronted with what the Bible has to say about the God who hears the cry of the poor, liberates the oppressed, and calls us to be passionately involved in the struggle for justice, I have also begun to envision a new future for my country as it discovers how to use its wealth and power in the pursuit of these same goals and thus helps to construct a new international order of greater stability and peace.

I have been encouraged to find that many women and men I meet in the U.S.A., especially in church circles, are concerned about these same issues. They have made an effort to inform themselves about Central America through reading, participation in study groups, and listening to reports of those who have visited or lived there. Many of them have had contact with Central Americans living in our midst who are refugees from the violence in El Salvador or Guatemala. Some have traveled to Central America or other countries caught up today in social upheavals. As a result of these experiences, they too have become disturbed by the poverty and suffering, the injustice and exploitation, of which they are now aware, and are shocked to discover how little attention is given to these matters by those responsible for articulating and defending present policies.

Many of them have also been influenced by the witness of Third World Christians. They have often been astonished by the vitality of faith and depth of commitment of men and women they have met, and by their interpretation of the Bible. On numerous occasions, those who have had this experience have told me that they have taken up the Bible again with new interest, and have been quite surprised by what they have found in it. They have also spoken of their desire to have something that would help them establish an ongoing dialogue between the Bible and the issues with which they are now struggling related to U.S. policy toward Third World nations.

This book is my attempt to provide a resource for such reflection. I'm convinced that the Bible has something important to say about these matters. I've found that, over the years, it has contributed decisively to shaping my perspective on international relations and I see increasing evidence that the same thing is happening with others with similar concerns. And I believe the time has come for us to make a more concerted effort to explore what the Bible may have to say about the issues now claiming our attention.

I am not an expert in the field of international relations nor a biblical scholar. But I have spent more than four decades living and working in two worlds, the North and the South, and attempting to make sense of that experience through biblical and theological study and reflection. In presenting here the results of that effort, my main concern is not to convince the reader of the rightness of my position but rather to encourage you to carry on your own investigation and arrive at your own conclusions, taking into account a reading of the Bible that I believe deserves consideration.

In my search for a biblical orientation on issues central to U.S. policy toward the Third World, I have focussed primarily on the Exodus and the writings of the prophets in the Old Testament, and on the Gospels and, to a limited extent, on the Pauline Epistles in the New Testament. I have done this because I find that these texts express what to me is most central to Christian faith and contribute to the articulation of a perspective that speaks clearly and convincingly regarding some of the issues before us. I realize that, in doing this, I have not taken into account other possible lines of thought in the Bible, and that there is no way I can prove that my interpretation of the biblical story is the correct one. But I'm convinced that the power of the biblical Word lies in part in its capacity, time and again, to speak a new word in a new situation, a word that commends itself because of its compelling nature, a word the truth of which can be demonstrated only as it is lived out over the years. I have seen this happen as the Bible is read by the poor in Latin America, and I believe that it will happen on the frontiers of our struggles in this country as well.

I have attempted to probe as deeply as possible into what the Bible has to say on the issues under discussion and to suggest some possible implications of it for our relations as a nation with developments now taking place in Latin America and elsewhere. But I have not tried to formulate principles and deduce from them, in a strictly logical way, what each might mean for national policy. During my years of teaching in seminary, I came to realize that the logical arrangement of concepts may not contribute very much to opening our minds to new truth, transforming our values, or leading us to respond to imperatives. On the other hand, as I have participated in Christian base communities in Latin America I have frequently experienced another process of perceiving and appropriating truth. As men and women living in concrete situations of struggle and committed to following Christ have studied the Bible together in community, the Holy Spirit has led them into rich insight as to the meaning of that word as well as sacrificial action in response to it. It is my hope that these chapters will encourage small groups here to explore a similar process.

This book is directed especially to those who find that their religious faith is leading them to undertake a re-examination of U.S. policy. I trust it will be of interest to others who take the Bible to be God's Word but have not been concerned about how that Word might transform their views on foreign policy matters. And I hope it will also further dialogue with those who are disturbed by what they see their country doing in Central America and elsewhere but have no particular religious interest. I have found that the Bible has a way of addressing us and laying a claim upon us, even when we don't start out from a clearly articulated belief in its authority. There is, I believe, something about what it has to say on such issues that not only makes sense but can also stimulate us to move beyond where we now are in our thought and action.

# INTRODUCTION

WITH THE VIETNAM WAR, the problem of U.S. relations with
Third World countries broke into our national consciousness, and
since that time it has not gone away. We live in a constant state of
uneasiness, uncertain as to when or where we will be caught up in
another crisis. Lebanon and Libya, the Persian Gulf and Iran, the
Philippines, South Africa and Central America: all these conjure
up images of conflict. We are now well aware that many nations
of Asia, Africa, and Latin America face tremendous economic and
political problems, problems that seem to defy solution and get
worse year by year. We also know that what is happening in each
of these countries affects us, and that what we do as a nation has
a profound impact on them.

In the last few years, all of this has come to a focus in Central America. This is partly because El Salvador, Nicaragua, and
Guatemala are so very close to the U.S.A. But our concern about
the area has been intensified by the attention given to it and the
assertions made about it by those in high positions in government
and in the media. In a speech given on April 27, 1983, President
Reagan declared that "the national security of all the Americas is
at stake in Central America." A year later, the *Wall Street Journal*
identified Central America as "the number one priority on the foreign policy agenda," more important than arms control, the MX
missiles, or even Star Wars (Editorial, November 15, 1984). And
the report of the Kissinger Commission called it the "geo-strategic
crossroads of the world with global dimensions."

The congressional hearings on the Iran-*contra* affair focus our
attention even more sharply on Third World issues. The hearings underline one thing that has been clear from the start: Those
involved in these ventures were convinced that dangerous develop-

1

ments in the Third World called for decisive action on the part of the United States, action so urgent that it had to be done covertly, outside the normal bureaucratic structures. The exposure of their naiveté and of the failure of their efforts should convince us not only of the seriousness and complexity of the problems we face but also of the bankruptcy of outmoded solutions and the need for new perspectives. We can rejoice that we live in an open democratic society in which such antidemocratic ventures can be exposed and rejected. But we should also realize that we will be able to preserve such a society and guarantee that our thought and action as citizens continue to play a role in shaping national policy only as we make maximum use of the freedoms and rights we enjoy.

One of the most vigorous responses to this challenge is now coming from segments of the Christian community. They are demonstrating that our religious heritage is capable of leading people to study foreign policy issues, come up with alternatives to present policy, and struggle to bring about changes in line with their vision. Their faith has not provided them with a neat set of principles or with a political program, but it has offered them a perspective on life and the world from which to assess what is happening around them and thus perceive more clearly what our nation can and should be doing in relation to other nations.

The reason for this is not hard to find. At the center of Christian faith is Jesus Christ, the Redeemer, the Liberator. Thus the world is seen as a realm in which redemption is taking place. The history of the world is the story of the struggle of oppressed people for liberation and life. Faith in God carries with it confidence in a Divine Presence calling us to transform the world in the direction of the Reign of God, a new order of justice and peace. Consequently, human communities and nations can find meaning and purpose in their existence and enjoy peace and stability only as they strive toward this end.

This fundamental conviction, this vision of what is happening in the world and in history, has a number of important consequences for our reflection on international relations and sets certain terms for our thought and action:

1. Confidence in the presence of God in the concrete historical struggles of people frees us to look realistically at what is happening around us. We need not be afraid of it or try to hide from it. In fact, if we believe in and yearn for the transformation of

the world, then we must make a special effort to understand what stands in the way of it and how these obstacles can be overcome. And we will be especially attuned to efforts or movements capable of carrying society beyond the dead ends in which it is caught.

2. Those in positions of power, who define and carry out U.S. policy, may be inclined to think in geopolitical terms, convinced that their primary responsibility is to preserve U.S. power and influence. Faith focuses on people, especially those who are deprived of full life; it leads us to concern ourselves primarily about them and their needs, and how our policy affects them.

I got a new sense of what this means while speaking recently with a woman in her seventies, from a conservative small town in upper New York State. Some months earlier she had spent two weeks in Central America with a group from her church, her first trip outside the U.S.A. That experience had transformed her life and led her to travel widely, speaking in churches about her experience. In our conversation, she said that she knew little about theology or international affairs but she did know that her Christian faith had always led her to be concerned about people who were suffering. And then she said: "When I think about Central America now, I think of peasants describing how wealthy landlords forced them off the little plots of land their families had owned for generations, depriving them of their only means of subsistence; a poor Salvadoran woman in a refugee camp telling us how 'uniformed men' went to her house and killed her husband and two sons after they started to organize a small farmers' cooperative, and Delegates of the Word in rural Nicaragua telling us how the *contra* bands come to their villages and rape, torture, and often kidnap or kill the grassroots leaders who are working at adult education, health care, or agricultural development." She also assumed, as I discovered later, that it is in our national self-interest to take this into account.

3. Anyone can, of course, use the Bible to support and try to give a sacred aura to his or her own prejudices. But by taking the Bible as our point of reference, we also have the possibility of doing something quite radical, looking at our foreign policy from a perspective that transcends the limitations of our narrow ideological worldview and is capable of calling our policies into question. For the Bible challenges us to put together our story of who we are and where we are going as a nation in dialogue with the story

of the struggle of another people. When we do this, we may find that our struggle takes on new meaning as our horizons expand; we may also realize that, in the context of faith, understanding leads inevitably to action.

In my attempt to reflect on U.S. policy in the Third World from this vantage point, I begin by looking at some of the new developments that have taken place during the last several decades that create a new situation for the U.S.A. In the second chapter, I develop the thesis that some of these developments may be much more closely related than we think to our own history and ideals, having been stimulated by our presence and what we have stood for in these countries. If this is the case, then we have a much greater opportunity than we have imagined until now to relate creatively to them.

From there I proceed to explore four major issues which, from a biblical perspective, take on central importance, and on each of which I find that the Bible has a great deal to say:

- Our relation as a nation to the poor and marginal people who make up the vast majority of the inhabitants of the Third World.

- Our capacity, as a people traditionally oriented toward the future, to envision a new future for ourselves as well as for the people of other lands.

- Our fear of social revolutions and our opposition to the consolidation of new social orders, given the fact that our nation was born in a revolution and that we are now celebrating the two hundredth anniversary of our consolidation of a new society.

- The temptation of powerful nations to idolatry.

Two chapters have been given to the discussion of each issue: the first concentrating on biblical passages that speak directly or indirectly to that particular problem and may suggest a new or different approach to it; the second, reflecting on what it might mean for us as a nation to act more in line with such a perspective.

# Chapter 1

# THE CHALLENGE
# FROM THE PERIPHERY

O UR BELIEF IN OUR GOODNESS as a nation makes it very difficult for us to understand why we face a serious challenge from the people and nations of the Third World. We know that we have tremendous economic and military power, but we don't want to be called imperialists; we believe that we use our power to serve the cause of freedom and democracy, not for the sake of domination over other nations. We are well aware that because of our economic resources, technological know-how, and material wealth we stand out over the rest of the world; yet we are convinced that we use all this to serve the interests not only of ourselves but of other nations as well. We want to be liked by other people; we also want to feel secure. And, as befits the citizens of such a powerful nation, we assume that along with the burdens, responsibilities, and risks we face, we also deserve to receive some special benefits as well.

Moreover, our experience at the end of the Second World War dramatically reinforced these convictions about ourselves and our place in the world of nations. Henry Luce and others announced the advent of the American Century. We emerged from the war with the atomic bomb, giving us unchallenged military superiority. The economies of Japan, Russia, and the Western European nations had been devastated by the war; we had unprecedented economic wealth and power. The war brought an end to the Great Depression; with the war's end, we were sure we had entered an era of amazing economic growth that would all but eliminate poverty in America and equip us to help poorer nations around the world

5

improve the lot of their people. The world was once again under control, and we felt certain that we could use our power to keep it that way. We were proud to be North Americans, and we felt secure.

Before long, this picture began to change. The Soviet Union gradually came close to matching our nuclear capabilities and soon emerged as a second superpower, challenging our supremacy first in Europe and then in other parts of the world. Even more disturbing changes began to take place in the nations of Asia, Africa, and Latin America. As they struggled to free themselves from poverty and faced revolutionary upheavals, they began to articulate their longings for a new international economic order and greater political independence. A new generation of leaders in one country after another challenged our assumption that our economic relations with the Third World served their interests; some of them denounced us as the new imperialists. In reaction, our government tended to side even more than before with the small privileged minorities in these countries, against those working for change. But when we intervened militarily to keep things from getting out of control, the results were not what we expected.

In this regard, the war in Vietnam was the turning point. For the first time in our history, our nation was defeated militarily — by a guerrilla army made up of poorly armed peasants. Also for the first time, here at home, a growing number of men and women, young and old, began to raise fundamental ethical questions about how our power was being used around the world. With the taking and holding of the hostages in the American embassy in Tehran, we were forced to face the fact that we were no longer in control of a dangerous world. Our power seemed to be in precipitous decline; our national self-confidence had been rudely shaken.

President Reagan, together with those responsible for formulating and carrying out his foreign policy, is making a bold attempt to reverse this process. In their eyes, the U.S.A. has a historic mission in the world today, to defend freedom against its enemies, embodied above all in the agents of international Communism. They see the decline of our power in the recent past as due to a growing reluctance on the part of our leadership to flex our economic, political, and military muscles, and to the failure of the people of this nation to back it up.

For Reagan and his associates, this era of humiliation and

defeat has ended. With the invasion of Grenada, the escalation of U.S. intervention in Central America, and the overall military build-up, the tide has turned. Our policies are working; our power is more and more respected around the world, and Communist aggression is gradually losing the contest in Central America and elsewhere.

Reagan has demonstrated, so claim his supporters, that when the U.S. pursues its own national self-interest most vigorously it contributes most decisively to world stability and peace. The more far-reaching America's influence, the more stable will be the world and the safer the U.S.A. In the new international milieu created by these initiatives, we can once again have confidence in the relevance of our national experiment for the rest of the world. "The tide of history is with us"; the world is looking to us, to our economic system and our way of life, with expectation and hope.

This being the case, they say, our pride in our nation is being restored. We can once again feel good about being Americans and have confidence in the legitimacy and success of our institutions. Those who dare to question all this are looked upon as victims of a negative, "blame America" attitude and are frequently accused of being unpatriotic.

One problem, however, still remains, and all the efforts being made in Washington to ignore it are destined to fail. *While the U.S.A. is doing everything possible to shore up the old patterns of relationships, the people of the Third World have already begun a new era in which the continuation of such relationships is impossible.*

## An Axial Shift in North-South Relations

Five hundred years ago, the nations of Western Europe launched a movement that was destined to set the terms for relationships between the peoples of the world from that time until the present. They began an era of exploration and penetration, exploitation and domination, of three continents: Asia, Africa, and South America. Later on, the U.S.A. got in on the act and now plays a major role in maintaining that system.

As the Western nations extended their influence to the rest of the world, they took with them their culture and civilization, their political and economic structures. They also established a colonial system, combining political domination with economic exploitation, and were able to maintain it, by and large, well into the twentieth century. At the end of World War II, national movements for independence exploded and eventually succeeded in one country after another. But they were carried out by a small Westernized elite who, by and large, were unable to achieve economic independence or lay the foundations for a stable society serving the interest of the majority of the people.

Their success in challenging the colonial system along with their failure to provide an acceptable alternative to it has prepared the way for the new era now beginning. In it, the great majority of the people (who have been and still are desperately poor and excluded from participation in national life) are beginning to emerge and claim a place for themselves. And as they do so, they are joined by a significant number of men and women from the upper classes.

As these two groups come together, they realize that this situation of dehumanization and suffering is not decreed by God nor by Fate but is the product of an unjust economic and political order. They see that the vaunted Western-style economic development is not improving the lot of the majority, but impoverishing them even more. They find themselves a part of more than one billion people who today do not have sufficient food, decent housing, or adequate medical care. And they also know that the situation they face will only get worse, unless they act to change it.

In response to this challenge, a new movement is taking place around the world that may be of as great historical importance as the Western conquest. *The poor people and those who stand with them are emerging as the new HISTORICAL SUBJECTS, taking the lead in creating a new society. They are launching grassroots popular movements in which they are discovering their own worth and power. They are determined to liberate themselves from the oppression under which they are suffering.* They now realize that they can have a decent human life only as they have increasing control over their destiny. They are willing to struggle, and if necessary die, to achieve that goal.

In some countries, these movements are in their initial stages; in others they are well advanced. But at whatever stage they are, they are articulating a vision of a *new democratic society*, inspired in part by us and our heritage but shaped in response to their situation.

Three elements of this vision stand out:

- An economic order oriented around using the resources of the nation to meet the most basic needs of the great majority of the people;

- New political structures in which people in local communities can have more and more control over their life and destiny, and in which the exercise of power moves increasingly from the bottom up rather than from the top down;

- International nonalignment, by means of which the smaller and poorer nations have the opportunity to develop relations of mutual support, economically and politically, with each other and, from this base, restructure their relationships with the more powerful nations of the world.

North Americans may be shocked to realize that many of the leaders in this struggle get much of their inspiration and orientation from Western religious movements and political ideologies that they have adapted to their situation. In a number of countries, especially in Latin America, a new generation of Christians are among those in the forefront. Many of them belong to the new professional elite we have helped to train: brought up in churches we helped to establish and educated in our colleges and universities. Others, who often constitute the mass base of movements for change, are poor peasants and slum dwellers whose lives have been transformed by reading the Bible and living together in a community of faith. They have found, in the Hebrew and Christian Scriptures, a message of liberation from oppression that we rarely hear. Their faith sustains them and often leads them to risk their lives for that cause.

A new generation of men and women influenced by Marxism often has a vision and commitment quite similar to that of the Christians. In some parts of the Third World, their appeal to the masses cannot compare to that of the Christians, but their influence is a major force for change.

What distinguishes many of them from a former generation of revolutionaries is their sensitivity to the history, culture, and people of their own countries. As a result of this, they have no desire to be obedient subjects of an international Communist movement directed by the Soviet Union. They are much more concerned to find authentic solutions to their own national problems than to develop and impose the right ideological line. They too envision a society in which the poor will find new life as they have a chance to participate in the exercise of public power. Their Marxism is becoming more humanistic and less doctrinaire.

## The Growing Disillusionment with U.S. Policy

These men and women, whatever their religious or ideological orientation, whether they be poor or rich, are concerned about the suffering of the great majority of poor people: their anguish because they are hungry and their children are starving; the fact that, if their children get sick, they may die because their parents can't take them to a doctor or buy medicine for them; the miserable conditions under which they live their lives; the fact that they have no place in society and little or no chance of improving their lot. They are dedicated, above all else, to bringing about a change in this situation. They look to our country in the hope that we can face that challenge and be willing to change our traditional policies in response to a new situation. But most of what they see the U.S.A. doing leads them to the conclusion that we are quite unconcerned about this suffering; more than that, they see that what we are doing contributes, in many cases, to making their situation worse.

Time and again we give economic and military support to a very small ruling class that has almost complete control of the government and the economy and uses that power to get richer at the expense of the majority. We, of course, benefit from this arrangement for these countries purchase consumer goods we produce; the rulers also make it possible for our corporations to find cheap labor without being disturbed by worker protests.

In recent years, the value of exports from many Third World countries has declined, while our massive expenditures for the military have led to higher interest rates that now impose a heavy burden on their economies. At the same time, when they most need money for economic development, U.S. banks have reduced their loans from $50 billion in 1981 to $20 billion in 1982, to $10 billion in 1983. And the International Monetary Fund imposes, as conditions for help, the devaluation of the currency, reductions in public spending, and control of inflation by holding down wages. As a result, a larger percentage of the poor majority are unemployed or underemployed, and so less able to meet their most elementary needs.

Under these conditions, social unrest grows. Those in power try desperately to maintain the status quo by repression. In one country after another, expressions of dissatisfaction, movements of public protest, and efforts on the part of the poor to organize for political action are met with arrests, torture, and, in some cases, "disappearances." And, time and time again, the U.S.A. is involved in supporting this whole process and providing more and more military support for those in power. We end up giving little or no economic aid to countries attempting to redirect their economies toward greater national self-reliance and redistribution of wealth.

At the same time, we pour more and more money into military support for the status quo. During the year 1984, for example, our opposition to Nicaragua deprived the people of about $200 million in foreign aid and forced them to spend 25 percent of their gross national product on defense. Meanwhile we spent more than $500 million on military support to El Salvador. Moreover, our support for reactionary regimes helps sustain their policy of arresting, forcing into exile, or killing many of the men and women whose vision and commitment could make a major contribution to social stability and peace through economic development serving the interest of the people.

## The Injury We Inflict on Ourselves

We cannot pursue a policy for long that runs counter to the dynamic movements occurring among Third World people without doing immense damage not only to them but to ourselves as a people as well. Already we can see clear signs of the injury we are doing to ourselves.

1. With all of our military expenditures and interventions in Third World countries, we have accomplished very little. According to the estimates of one diplomatic historian, we have spent more than 100 billion dollars in the pursuit of our goals in these countries since World War II, yet the stability and peace we aim for seems to be farther and farther away. Our nation has intervened

more than two hundred times in other nations, yet the process we are following seems to call for more such involvement, not less, as the years go on. Our intervention in Guatemala in 1954 set in motion a process of destabilization of the country that has continued until recent times. Our involvement in the overthrow of the Allende regime in Chile in 1973, and our support of the military government of Pinochet, have led to economic disaster, incredible violation of human rights, and growing discontent. So much so that now, fifteen years after the Pinochet government came to power, people are so desperate that not even violent repression will contain them. Judged by its results, the policy we have been following helps to create increasingly unstable social and political situations, which then depend more and more on U.S. power to shore them up.

2. Our present policy is justified on the ground that it will make us feel secure and safe here at home; thus far, the results are the opposite. A policy that does not face or resolve the fundamental problems causing insecurity around the world can only end up making us more insecure. Our increasing intervention in Nicaragua helps to unite people in that country against us and brings them more support from other Latin American countries. The nations of the Contadora group (Panama, Venezuela, Colombia, and Mexico) seek greater independence of the U.S.A. as we block their efforts to find a political solution to the problems of Central America. Our support of rightist dictators, who exploit the people of their own countries, can only lead to increasing hostility toward the U.S.A. And in a world in which we create such conditions for ourselves, we can only live in fear and insecurity, no matter how great our military might.

Obsession with military control of the world leads us to spend money on defense that is badly needed at home for economic development, for providing human services, offering people a chance to have decent housing, meaningful work, and economic security. When these things are sacrificed, we destroy the fabric of social life that makes our local communities safe and secure. And, as a nation and a people, we can only feel secure as we are engaged, along with the people of the Third World, in the creation of a society serving the interests of all. When we are concerned only about maintaining our own power and wealth — over against a starving world — we lose the vision and the commitment to a common cause that could give meaning to our existence as a nation in the new era we are now entering.

3. Love of country and strong patriotic sentiments are good. But they can be a positive force and play a positive role in the world only as they are built on a solid foundation, only if they are a contemporary expression of the values by which we as a nation have lived.

Our nation was born in a revolution in which we demanded independence from Great Britain. For two hundred years, we have been a symbol to the colonized nations of the world of something they also hope to achieve someday for themselves. Yet, at the present time, we are blocking their efforts to gain such independence. During the Truman presidency, orders were given to remove the Declaration of Independence from the overseas libraries maintained by the U.S.A. because of its possible incendiary influence. More recently, our interventions are even more blatant denials of what we most cherish as a nation.

We have taken great pride in our nation as one where considerations of rank and privilege are downplayed and "the common man" has a chance to come to center stage. As we lived this out in the past, we challenged other nations as well to follow this path. I remember a conversation I had years ago with Professor Carl Friedrich at Harvard, who came to this country from Germany at the beginning of the Hitler era. Reminiscing on what his coming to America had meant, he said that above all else, it represented a conversion to a belief in "the common man" on the part of someone brought up to believe in the elite. Today, the "common people" of Third World countries, the poor, are not only captivated by this same vision as it applies to them; they are willing to struggle to transform their societies in that direction. Yet, all too often, they see the U.S.A. as the major force in the world working against them. Sooner or later, the common people of this country will have to face what they are doing to the common people of the world. If we continue to get involved in military actions in which our soldiers are killing defenseless peasants — often Christian leaders dedicated to raising up those who are most downtrodden — they will sooner or later be devastated by the contradiction between what they are doing and the ideals that inspire them as human beings and as North Americans.

### The Challenge before Us

The problem we face has not been caused primarily by international Communism, Third World intransigence, or the upsurge of revolutionary movements. It is a problem we have in large part created for ourselves, by our inability to change our policy in response to a new historical situation. The crisis in which we are caught is due not to any lack of alternatives to our present policy but to our lack of imagination and will to invent and carry out new policies. The challenge before us is to begin to envision a new world order and to work toward changes in our relationships with Third World countries that will take more seriously their struggle for national self-determination. As we do this, we will be able to explore new patterns of economic and political relations and thus create conditions for greater stability and peace. But this road to the future can only be explored if we are willing to look critically at the policies we have been following as well as the assumptions on which they have been based. What is called for is a willingness to re-examine our place in the world of nations and come to a new understanding of the contribution we can bring to the survival and well-being of all people in an interdependent world.

This presents a challenge that cannot easily be met by those who now shape our policy. Our foreign policy establishment shows little interest in seeking new solutions to the problems they face; their concern is usually a very pragmatic one, how to solve immediate problems in a way that will serve narrow U.S. interests of the moment, that is, keep us from losing influence and if possible gain more power for us. Questions raised about the validity of basic assumptions underlying our policy are dismissed as "ideological." Such a limited view of national self-interest means that time and again they claim privileges for our country that deny the most basic rights of other nations. We can intervene in El Salvador or Nicaragua at will, at the same time that we denounce even the possibility of others doing the same. For two centuries, we have espoused the right of national self-determination for ourselves; we now deny it to others.

In my contacts over the years with State Department officials, at home and abroad, I have been astonished to see how little those who make and carry out our policy are interested in data that does not fit their narrow picture, or in engaging in dialogue with those representing opposing points of view. They are largely isolated from the poor who are victims of our policy, and thus can make decisions far removed from the human reality affected by them. All too often, their concern for national self-interest is subordinate to concern for the power and influence of their own section of the bureaucracy, and the enhancement of their own personal position within it.

In the political arena, the debate about our policy is all too narrowly defined. By and large, liberals and conservatives, Republicans and Democrats, operate on the same basic assumptions in regard to our relations to the Third World. They assume that our economic system and way of life, together with our economic involvement in poor countries and some small amount of economic assistance, will contribute significantly to their economic development and to overcoming poverty. Liberals as well as conservatives fear revolutionary instability, assuming that it must be caused by foreign influences and will lead inevitably to communism. Both groups tend to favor the use of military force to intervene in order to avoid radical social change. As a result, there is, at present, no significant political force in Congress or the nation capable of challenging old clichés, making a more realistic analysis of the complex situation and the variety of options open in the struggle for economic and social change in the Third World. Consequently, there is no political base for public debate, for the articulation of new approaches or the development of public support for them.

Given this situation, we can hope to move ahead only as small groups of concerned men and women get together all across the country to study the problem in greater depth, develop new perspectives on it, and constitute a base for ongoing education and action.

# Chapter 2

# THE UNFINISHED REVOLUTION
# IN INTERNATIONAL RELATIONS

CONFRONTED BY THE DEMANDS of Third World peoples for fundamental changes in our relationships with them, we often assume that they reject our values and want to destroy the way of life we cherish. If they use Marxist language and are favorably inclined toward socialism, we're sure they are our enemies. And when our political leaders play on these fears and denounce those who challenge us as evil, our worst suspicions are confirmed.

If, however, we listen to what the more progressive Third World leaders are saying, we often find that they honor the very ideals we preach. They admit that they have been profoundly influenced by them and may insist that they are trying to put them into practice in their situation. Moreover, by taking this position, they are affirming something that has been going on for a long time. The Wilsonian democratic vision appealed to many in Asia and inspired a movement for national liberation in Korea. The Four Freedoms proclaimed by the Allied nations during World War II encouraged the struggles for national independence in many parts of Asia and Africa. And even among a new generation of revolutionary leaders, there are many who admit that they have been influenced by Western and Christian ideals. In my contacts over the years with those working for radical change in various Third World countries, I have been amazed by their frequent references to Western social and political thought, to the importance of their early education in Christian schools and their study of the Bible.

This is, of course, only part of the picture. Western colonial expansion meant the brutal treatment of indigenous people, the exploitation of three continents for the enrichment of the West, and the undermining if not the destruction of cultures that had sustained societies for many centuries. The missionary movement played an important role in sustaining this Western penetration. Today, the whole world is paying a high price for all this, and a central element in the struggle of Third World peoples is their attempt to create a new and authentic life for themselves as they strive for greater cultural, as well as economic and political, independence. If we as a nation block their efforts to achieve this goal, they may well go much further than they have until now in their rejection of what we stand for.

At the present time, however, I'm convinced that some of the things we value most in our Western and Christian heritage now occupy a central place in the lives and struggles of Third World peoples. As diverse histories and cultures have come together and interacted, certain perspectives on life and the world have not only emerged but are now almost taken for granted around the world. Once we realize this fact, we can see that we North Americans and many Third World peoples not only have more in common than we have thought; *we and they are striving for similar goals.*

If we do not see eye to eye, it could be because they have taken the ideals we cherish more seriously than we have and are daring to follow through on them. In other words, they may be insisting on finishing the revolution we started but have not had the will to complete. To the extent that this is the case, the challenge they present to us is above all else to face the implications of our own preaching, to take more seriously our own heritage and allow it to be re-created in response to a new historical situation.

## The Western Worldview

Here I would like to identify five elements that make up our modern worldview and show what they now mean for many men and women in the Third World. In doing this, I am not trying to claim that they are exclusively Western or Christian or emphasize pride of ownership. At this point the important thing is for us to realize that they have a central place in our own history. Whatever place they originally had, or did not have, in other cultures, today they represent a dynamic force in the interaction of nations. If we realize that these elements in our worldview have not only shaped us but are now accepted around the world, we will be able to hope and work for a new international order. For those of us who take our orientation from our Christian faith, the recognition of their religious source can contribute significantly to further reflection on our responsibility in the world of nations.

1. *We are convinced that human life — the life of every human being as it is lived in the here and now — is of ultimate importance. Consequently, all human thought, energy, and activity should be dedicated to the task of creating conditions for human fulfillment here and now.*

All of this makes sense because history is the arena in which the human struggle for redemption is taking place. Human life in history is moving toward greater fulfillment. Whatever the specific obstacles to it existing in any time and place, they can be overcome. The transformation of life and society is possible, and well worth all the effort given to it.

Most of us are so accustomed to look at life and history this way that it doesn't strike us at all as revolutionary. I realized its importance only after coming in contact with people, cultures, and worldviews oriented in a very different direction: where a sharp distinction was made between the earthly, material, temporal world and a higher spiritual order; where human longings and desires were seen as illusions or evils to be overcome; where tremendous human energies were spent in the search for spiritual peace and security, apparently far removed from what I understood as the *real world.*

If there is something in our society that compels us to be concerned about social injustice and leads us to believe that the world can be transformed, certainly our Judeo-Christian tradition is one of the principal sources of it. The Old Testament portrays a God constantly active in history; a God who called a people into existence, led them out of Egypt, and established them as a nation with a special mission in history. This God gives ultimate importance to relationship with this people, and to their relationship with each other. The cyclical approach to history has been broken, for Yahweh has a goal for human life on earth and is moving toward it in spite of all human limitations and failures.

The New Testament adds another dimension to this with its claim that, in Jesus of Nazareth, God became *incarnate.* God takes on human flesh, enters into the material world and the historical struggle. We no longer need to strive to rise above the material world to encounter the transcendent. God meets us here. Human life is of ultimate importance; the Reign of God as the divine goal for human existence is taking shape within history through the transformation of human relationships and social structures.

When we step outside our own nation and culture, we can see more clearly the injustices perpetrated by Western civilization as well as the failure of the church to live up to the message it proclaims; at the same time, we become much more aware of the revolutionary impact that this approach to historical existence has on other peoples.

2. *We believe there is a radical separation of the divine from the human as well as the cosmic order, resulting in the desacralization of nature and society.*

In the early 1960s, a Dutch theologian, Arend van Leeuwen, published a book entitled *Christianity in World History,* which attracted a great deal of attention not only in religious circles but beyond them as well. In it, he claimed that ancient cultures, as well as traditional societies in Asia and Africa, were *ontocratic* in character. They conceived of reality as one cosmic totality, in which the divine was so much an integral part of nature and society as to give them a sacral character. A mystical power hovered over these two realms. Men and women often lived in fear of nature and dared not tamper with it. Kings and other rulers belonged to the divine order. Their power as well as the laws by which they ruled had something sacred about them; the institutions and structures of the status quo were thus exempt from attack.

For van Leeuwen, the faith of Israel represented a radical break with this entire ontocratic system. Belief in God as the Creator meant discontinuity between the divine and the realms of nature and society. And as this approach was incorporated into Christianity and was worked out in the Western world, it led inevitably to a process of secularization that gradually made its influence felt on all continents.

As a result, the way was paved for scientific investigation. The natural order could be explored not only to discover its secrets but to harness it to the service of human beings. In the same way, the social order was desacralized. Economic, social, and political structures were seen as human creations, to be analyzed, criticized, and changed when necessary. Society was conceived of as a "project," to be created by human will and action, not as an eternal order, claiming divine authority.

In developing this thesis, Professor van Leeuwen may have exaggerated the difference between Western and other cultures. But he focussed attention on one of the most dynamic forces at work in the world today and highlighted the contribution made to it by our Judeo-Christian heritage.

3. *With the expansion of the West, the isolation of traditional cultures was shattered. People everywhere were challenged to expand their world through the encounter with the historical experience of other nations and races, with science and technology as well as new ideas in other realms.* The international stage was thus set for a dynamic process of growth and mutual enrichment of all cultures.

Moreover, the West was inspired by the vision of *one world.* We assumed that all nations were destined to relate to each other in a movement toward unification. As nations moved out of their isolation, they would eventually overcome millennial hatreds leading toward war and participate in the creation of a global civilization.

Here, too, our religious tradition played a major role in articulating and sustaining this vision. For the people of Israel, Yahweh was the only God, Creator of the entire universe and Lord of all nations, a God whose will and purpose embraced all peoples of the earth. This radical monotheism laid the foundation for our global vision.

Later, the prophets of the Old Testament added new dimensions and depth to it. Yahweh, for them, was the God of justice, who judged all nations by the same standard and willed to bring all peoples together in a messianic age in which the lion and the lamb would lie down together and nations would no longer war against each other. Jesus of Nazareth followed this prophetic line when he not only proclaimed this Reign of God as a world-embracing reality but announced that the new age it represented had already begun.

The early Christians expressed this vision in their doctrine as they conceived of the cosmic Christ reconciling the world to himself and creating a new people to carry forward this ministry of universal reconciliation. And as the missionary movement carried the church to the ends of the world, an international community began to take shape. Christians began to think in *ecumenical* terms, with a vision of unity embracing the whole inhabited world.

When we think of this vision of earlier generations, we realize how insensitive they were to the negative impact of Western expansion on other cultures; we can also perceive that the one world they envisioned was one largely dominated by the West, by its language and culture, its economic system and political institutions. The fact remains, however, that in and through this process, one generation after another of students and young professionals discovered a wider world and began to think in international terms. During several decades of association with the Student Christian Movement in Latin America, I saw this happen when young people from different countries met each other, shared their struggles and their dreams, came in contact with the people and the culture of other continents, and began to think in global terms.

4. *Our Western world has prided itself in the fact that it is oriented more toward the future than the past. We are inspired by a utopian vision rather than longing for the restoration of a past golden age. From the time of the Enlightenment until very recently, the idea of progress determined our understanding of historical process, and the extraordinary developments taking place in science and technology confirmed and gave concreteness to this article of faith.* This Western perspective, accompanied by ever-advancing technology, made a profound impact on all those nations and peoples it touched.

In many cultures, this meant a radical transformation in outlook. It broke the hold of the past over people who had always lived with a strong sense of historical continuity; it made it possible for men and women suffering under unjust and exploitative social systems to believe that their situation could be changed and to dream of a better future. It set the stage for human creativity to flourish.

This orientation toward the future has been especially strong in North America. Our nation never knew the heavy weight of tradition as in Europe, and our movement as a people toward an ever-expanding frontier strengthened even more our sense that we were constantly engaged in creating a better future. Consequently, utopian vision was an especially strong element in our cultural impact on the rest of the world.

The secular idea of progress, together with the dominant influence of science and technology, tended to obscure the fact that our religious heritage had been the primary source of this revolutionary change in our perception of historical existence. As a matter of fact, this orientation toward the future occupies a central place in the Hebrew and Christian Scriptures from beginning to end. The nation of Israel begins when Yahweh calls a slave people to leave Egypt and embark on a journey toward a land of promise; the prophets dream of a future messianic age and bring that yearning into the center of life of a conquered people. Jesus of Nazareth focuses attention on a new future already impinging upon the present. For the early Christians, the Christ who had been killed and resurrected would come again; with this expectation, they learned to look at the present moment eschatologically — in the light of the end toward which history is moving. Little wonder that, time and again in Christian history, men and women captivated by this vision have come together in new religious and social movements dedicated to the construction of a new order.

5. *Integral to the self-understanding of the church, from apostolic times onward, was the idea that it was called into existence not only to proclaim a new order but also to make that new order a reality through its own life as a community. It conceived of itself as a sign pointing to what was possible in the wider world.* After the church came to occupy an established position within Western Christendom, it performed a quite different function. But the vision was not entirely lost and reappeared frequently in monastic and sectarian movements.

As the missionary enterprise spread around the world into non-Western cultures, it once again made a significant contribution to social transformation, even when its protagonists were not aware of all that they were doing. In many areas, the church they established was small and relatively isolated from the larger society. But in conjunction with mission institutions dedicated to education and other forms of service, its presence contributed significantly to the impact, made by the perspectives we presented above, upon other cultures. By laying the foundation for the ecumenical movement, the missionary enterprise established new contacts and relationships among people, not only between the colonizers and the colonized, but also between one part and another of what is now called the Third World.

### Disturbing Implications of the Ideals We Proclaim

If so many of the things we most cherish in our cultural heritage are gaining wider and wider acceptance around the world, why then do we feel so threatened by what is happening? I'm convinced that one of the reasons is this: Under the impact of the West, people in other parts of the world have not simply appropriated something from abroad. They have interacted with it, in their situation of poverty and oppression, and in doing so, they have become aware of elements in it that we never perceived. As they have been transformed, they have discovered what it means to live an ongoing process of transformation. They now call upon us to do the same for the sake of our future as well as theirs.

I first became aware of this in a seminar with a group of African students at Princeton. They spoke eloquently about how Western and Christian influences had disrupted their traditional ways of life and had forced them to undergo the most radical changes. But they added: What the colonial powers and the missionaries did to humiliate and exploit us led us to see clearly that your way of life was as much in need of transformation as ours. More than that, we discovered that the religion you taught us was, in its very essence, a call for ongoing transformation, a message you presented to us but never applied to yourselves. Now we can say to you: The problem with what you did is not that you disrupted our way of life; it is rather that you preached a Gospel of Transformation which you never allowed to disrupt and change your world. All we are now doing is to ask you to face up to the implications of your own preaching.

If we look more closely at the five developments mentioned earlier in this chapter, we can get a better idea of the way in which contemporary Third World aspirations carry forward some of the things we have affirmed most vigorously.

1. *The Western obsession with what happens within history has gained almost universal acceptance.* Some of us in this part of the world may be drawn to religions offering us an escape from the burden of history; Third World people by and large are increasingly concerned about the elemental needs and realities of earthly existence. And their concern has dimensions to it that may take us by surprise.

Our bureaucratic and technocratic society tends to obscure the personal and the human, to cut us off from direct personal relationships. In the Third World, a new awareness of historical reality leads to greater awareness of the human, a concern for people. This in turn means a discovery of the concrete situation in which the majority of people live: that of extreme poverty and hunger, economic exploitation and political domination that denies them any place in society or any sense of their own worth.

Historical existence has a very concrete structure, which allows an extremely small minority to own the best land, control the economy, have almost total political power, and use all this to serve their own interests. As a result, preoccupation with historical existence leads to a passionate longing to overcome the present order and create conditions that make it possible for the great majority of human beings to enjoy a full human life.

When men and women in this situation read the Hebrew and Christian Scriptures, they make some amazing discoveries. They perceive that the God revealed there is on the side of the poor and acts dynamically in history to liberate them from exploitation and oppression. In fact, as the poor read the Bible, they realize that it is their book, that it tells their story. The central theme of the Old Testament is the Exodus of a slave people from Egypt in response to a call from this God, who then leads them to struggle to create an egalitarian and antiauthoritarian society in Canaan. The central passion of the Hebrew prophets is that of justice for the poor; they go so far as to declare that God judges all nations of the world on the basis of their response to the cry of the poor. In the New Testament, Jesus of Nazareth is presented to us as the incarnation of this God in a poor person, present in history to establish a Reign of justice and peace, in which the poor will occupy a privileged position. Consequently, concern for historical existence can lead those who are privileged to change sides and stand with the poor, while those who are underneath discover not only their own worth but their vocation at the center of history.

2. *The process of desacralization of the cosmic order and of society has proceeded apace. As it happens, many people in the Third World draw a conclusion we have not dared to face: this process means social revolution.*

Once the sacred aura enveloping society evaporates, the closed world in which the individual person has been encased is broken open, and that individual emerges with a clearer and stronger self-identity. Exploited people no longer need think of themselves as helpless victims of Fate; they no longer believe that their suffering is ordained by God. As the traditional religious worldview loses its hold over them, the most powerful force "keeping them in their place" is eroded. Oppressed peoples are free to become protagonists in the struggle for liberation.

At the same time, the established order of injustice loses what has served for centuries as its most powerful base of support. If those on top are no longer an integral part of the divine order, their authority is inevitably undermined, no matter how slow the process by which it occurs. Once this religious mystique surrounding them is gone, those whom they exploit will no longer be willingly submissive.

In our Western world, the process of secularization, at least in its early stages, was not an end in itself. It broke open a new world to be explored, and the collapse of structures of authority, as has happened repeatedly in the past, led to an explosion of creativity among those who began to taste a new freedom. We should hardly be surprised when the same thing happens in Third World countries. And if the great majority of those who experience this new freedom are the most oppressed, then they are going to demand a radical transformation of the economic and political order. While this is happening among Third World people, our process of secularization has brought us to the threshold of nihilism; at the same time, our use of our economic, political, and military power around the world has created conditions favorable to us, which we are not enthusiastic about changing. Thus, our presence and influence in the Third World has awakened expectations and energies for transformation that we once knew but are in danger of losing.

As we look at what is happening in this area, we cannot ignore the role Christianity has played in it. Christian missionaries, and the churches they established, proclaimed their faith in a Creator God who exposed all other divinities and sacred objects as created by human hands. They challenged the religious aura that gave a sacred character to traditional cultures and sustained oppressive economic and political structures. And precisely within a Christian context, the ensuing process of secularization aimed at offering abundant life within history to all peoples.

In many countries, especially in Asia and the Middle East, the number of converts to Christianity was very small and the "young" church was made up of a few largely marginalized people. But that is by no means the whole picture. Christian preaching and teaching, especially as it was associated with the expansion of Western penetration around the world, reached and affected a much wider circle. The schools and colleges established by the missionaries may not have gained many converts, but they communicated very well this desacralizing approach to culture and society.

3. *The Western dream of all peoples living in dynamic interrelation with each other in one world has caught on everywhere. But for those who are victims of colonial and neocolonial economic and political domination, this one world can become a reality only as present relationships are transformed.*

This should hardly come as a surprise to us. The ideals of the Western world inevitably arouse a longing for national self-determination in all people. The natural corollary of our affirmation of the individual person, living within a free democratic society, is a vision of each nation of the world, whatever its size or economic conditions, having increasing control over its own life and destiny. This means that each nation should be free to discover the uniqueness of its own culture and history and to develop economic, social, and political structures that are the most authentic expressions of this way of life. It means economic development oriented toward the most effective use of the resources of each nation to meet the needs of its people, in other words, the maximum degree possible of national self-reliance. Within this frame of reference, the creation of *one world* depends upon overcoming the present domination of the less powerful peoples of the world by large and powerful nations in order to move toward international interdependence. It calls for a *new* international economic and political order in which weak nations are free to discover and develop those elements in their national life that can most strengthen them. At the same time, they must cooperate with each other to create the most favorable conditions for mutual give-and-take with the rich and powerful.

Here again, Christianity has played an important role. We preached monotheism; many Third World people discovered that this God, the Creator and Ruler of all nations, was the God of justice whose action was aimed at the liberation of all oppressed peoples. We proclaimed a gospel that taught men and women to practice love in their individual lives; in the Scriptures that we put in their hands they learned about a Christ who would judge *all nations* according to their response to the cry of the "least": the hungry, the naked, the sick and the imprisoned. When the Brazilian educator Paulo Freire speaks of the "ontological vocation" of every human being to be a Subject, taking charge of his or her own life and destiny, he has captured one of the most fundamental elements in our religious heritage, which, once applied to the individual, must lead sooner or later to an affirmation of national self-determination.

4. *Western penetration in the Third World disrupted traditional societies and helped break the hold of the past over the minds of the people; it turned their attention toward the, until then, unimagined future and stirred up in them the vision of a better material life and a new sense of self-worth in society.* Today, they surprise us because they take this future orientation more seriously than we do and draw conclusions from it that we have not drawn.

They realize that their past, with all the suffering it brought, was the product of certain economic and political structures. They also see that these structures are still largely intact and that the U.S.A. plays a major role in sustaining them. Whether it be in South Korea, Chile, or El Salvador, this fact stands out all too clearly. The future, about which we encouraged them to dream, can be achieved only if the present order is overcome, yet our country seems determined to prevent that from happening and may use its power to help overthrow regimes dedicated to creating a new society.

At the very time when the people of the Third World, influenced in part by us, envision a new future and are committed to the task of creating it — willing in fact to die for it — we seem to have lost that vision. We appear to them as a people in bondage to our past, incapable of dreaming of an alternative future and lacking the will to struggle for it. Among the political ideologies originating in the West, Marxism often stands out as the only one that takes seriously this future orientation.

At the same time, many Christians are drawing on the religious heritage we made available to them to orient their struggle for a new future and are discovering dimensions of it which we have never seen. They connect easily with the messianic vision of a new age in the prophets of the Old Testament and see how central this was for Jesus of Nazareth. They realize that, in the Old and New

Testaments, this messianic vision means, in the words of Mary the mother of Jesus, that the mighty will be put down while those at the bottom will be raised up; the rich will be sent away empty while the hungry will be filled with good things (Luke 1:52–53). Third World Christians understand what the Gospels have to say about the future Reign of God even now breaking into the present; they also realize that this Reign, according to Jesus, belongs especially to the poor.

Little wonder that Christians are often the ones who find themselves most at home in a situation calling for systemic social change or find that Marxism is the one political ideology that speaks about the things their religious faith has taught them to be concerned about: social injustice, the oppression and suffering of the poor, and the transformation of society.

5. *We can no longer assume that the "younger churches," established a century ago by Western missionaries, represent a reproduction of Western middle-class Christianity, an insignificant minority largely isolated from the major forces working for social change. In some places at least, the church provides a community in which members of the small educated elite are converted to the struggle for justice, and the poor receive, from their religious faith and grassroots communities, the orientation, education, and support that often make them the natural leaders of the people's struggle.*

If this new development is unexpected, it is by no means without precedent. The example that stands out in closest relation to our own history is the participation of Puritans in the English Revolution of 1648. In the latter part of the sixteenth century, the Reformation launched by John Calvin in Geneva spread to England. There, according to Michael Walzer in his study *The Revolution of the Saints,* the Puritan divines developed a perspective on society that desacralized the established order and looked toward the creation of a new and more just society. In the small Puritan communities, members of the emerging middle class found an ideology, a strategy, and a discipline for revolution that came to play a decisive role in the whole movement.

Today, the Christian base communities in Latin America and elsewhere are the most striking example of this same phenomenon as it is taking place among the poorest, primarily in Roman Catholic circles. In these small communities, peasants and the urban poor are learning to relate what is happening to them in society to the religious symbols that are at the center of their lives. They are discovering their own worth, their capacity to think and to act, and are sustained in their struggle by the life they share with each other in a community brought together around their religious faith. In this context, a vital religious faith leads them into the struggle for liberation, motivates their action, and prepares them to play what may well be an increasingly important role in these movements.

The implications of this development for U.S. policy toward the Third World can hardly be exaggerated. Those who shape our foreign policy tend to see this as primarily a political rather than a religious phenomenon, a way by which those working for revolution, especially the Marxists, use religion to serve their political ends. Nothing could be farther from the truth.

In the West, the process of secularization has led many of us to think of religion as quite peripheral to the life of people today. The resurgence of the religious Right leads us to look on it as a means by which those who are most frightened by crisis and insecurity can shore up all that is being called into question. What we don't realize is that the worldview of large numbers of the poor of the Third World is essentially religious, and so is the source of their orientation and strength for survival. More and more, it is precisely this religious orientation that sensitizes them to their oppression, offers them a basis for hope that they can do something to change it, and pushes them toward involvement in struggles for liberation.

Furthermore, it is this Christian identification with the struggles of the poor that is opening a new era in the missionary outreach of the church. Many of the "younger churches" are indeed quite small and marginal, but as Christians become involved in these struggles they enter into a new relationship of dialogue and solidarity with others. While their primary concern may not be to win large numbers of converts, they are creating conditions for a much wider interaction not only with the poor but with others as well. At the same time, the networks of relationship established by the missionary and ecumenical movements mean that what is happening among Third World Christians will be more and more present in our midst. Their witness, and our response to it, could have a decisive influence on our policy in the years ahead.

Chapter 3

# THE GOOD NEWS
# WE MAY NOT WANT TO HEAR

THE MOST DIFFICULT PROBLEM we face in our relations with Third World countries has to do with the fact that we are rich and most of them are poor. Many of us now realize how wide the gap is between our affluence and the poverty of the majority of men, women, and children living in Asia, Africa, and Latin America. We are also beginning to perceive that existing economic relations between our two worlds favor us more than them and for this reason are being called into question. And we know that in one interdependent world we will face increasing tension and conflict until this situation is changed.

For many of us, this is very bad news. It leaves us facing a hostile world in which we may have to rely on military means to maintain our position of privilege. We don't want to do that, but we suspect that any other solution could only mean great loss to us. We thus become quite pessimistic about the future, and fear that our children and grandchildren will be condemned to live in a more violent world while gradually losing many of the material advantages we now enjoy.

### The Bible's Message

At the same time, we Christians have in our possession a book we believe to be divinely inspired, which speaks of God's presence in the struggle of the poor, refers to their liberation as *Good News*, and declares that individuals and nations can have a full life only as they contribute in some way to the struggle for a full life for all people. Many of us, to be sure, have read the Bible for a long time without perceiving this. But in recent years a number of biblical scholars as well as the members of Christian base communities have done a great deal to call our attention to it. And in various parts of the world, this same message has broken through to small groups of men and women from the more privileged classes as they have read the Bible. When they have responded to it, their lives have been profoundly changed.

I first experienced this when I went to Nicaragua in 1984. During the months I was there, I met a number of women and men from well-to-do families who were committed to building a new society serving the interests of the poor majority and were working hard at that task, often in key positions in the government or in private organizations. To my surprise, I discovered that most of them had participated, during the 1970s, in weekend retreats sponsored by the Cursillo movement. In these retreats, they were encouraged to cultivate their spiritual life and to study the Bible. Their reading of the Bible opened their eyes to the incredible poverty around them and made them realize that the God in whom they believed was calling them to do something about it. Thus, their spiritual rebirth and their study of the Bible lead them to analyze what was happening in Nicaraguan society and become involved politically, in the hope of bringing about major social reforms. When they realized that all roads toward such change by political means were blocked by the Somozan dictatorship, they decided to support the revolutionary struggle. Along this road, they not only found a new life for themselves in solidarity with the poor in their struggle for justice but also chose to give up much of their wealth and live quite simply.

I have found this same spirit elsewhere in Latin America among those who are providing lay leadership for the Popular Church (*iglesia popular**). Many of those I have met are university graduates who have turned away from opportunities to advance their professional careers in order to serve the base communities and popular movements. They use their abilities and training in projects serving the poor in the areas of education and health care, eco-

---

*A term used in Latin America to refer to the church of the people or the church of the poor.

nomic development, and community organizing, living and working on a subsistence basis. They have changed sides and participate in the struggles of the poor, knowing that their work may be considered to be subversive and that their lives may be in danger.

Over the last several years, I have known or heard of a number of small communities here in the U.S.A. whose members are following the same path. They too are being profoundly transformed by a vital religious faith, the study of the Bible, and contact with the poor. And they, just as their Latin American counterparts, find that their lives have been enriched and are taking on greater meaning and they are beginning to look toward the future with hope.

The Bible makes this impact upon its readers for a very good reason: both the Hebrew and Christian Scriptures focus attention on the poor and their suffering, speak of a time when it will be overcome, and emphasize the moral responsibility of those who are not poor toward the dispossessed. This comes through in the Psalms of the Hebrew people and the parables of Jesus, in the historical accounts of the people of Israel and the witness of the early Christian communities. What we have here is not a set of moral principles we are exhorted to follow, but the declaration that God, who is the object of faith, is passionately concerned about those human beings who are most deprived, most marginal, most victimized by society. God loves and defends the poor because they are poor. God hears their cry, stands by their side, yearns for their liberation, and acts to set them free. In addition to this, the biblical writers speak of this God as the Creator of heaven and earth, present and active in history, a God who has a goal for history and is working to achieve it. Consequently, the fate of peoples and nations is determined by whether or not they are moving in this same direction of justice for the poor. A brief look at the story of the Exodus, the thought of the Hebrew prophets, and the Gospels can give us some idea of how the biblical writers present and develop this unusual perspective.

The Exodus from Egypt is not only the central event in the formation of Israel as a nation; the Old Testament writers claim that in it the normative revelation of God has occurred. In this event, we can understand who the God of Israel is as well as God's purpose for this people and for all nations. But Yahweh appears here not as the God of the rich and powerful, defending the interests of the emperors of Egypt, but as the liberator of their slaves, a people sorely oppressed, "broken in spirit," and facing the possibility of extermination through forced labor projects and infanticide. God calls upon the Israelites to rebel and leads them out of Egypt toward a promised land. God's purpose in so acting is to weld a marginalized people into a new nation, living a new quality of life in community as they organize their economy along essentially egalitarian lines and go beyond oppressive structures of domination. Thus, the vocation of Israel as the servant of Yahweh is so to structure all aspects of its life that this liberation of the poor will become a historical reality and serve as a light to other nations.

Gradually, however, Israel became like other nations and abandoned its calling. With the establishment of kingship came greater centralization of power at the top; as the economy expanded the divine command to care for the poor was forgotten. Yahweh, the liberator of slaves, was worshipped by the wealthy and powerful, and the nation faced a series of internal crises and repeated attacks from external enemies.

In this situation, from the eighth to the sixth centuries before Christ, the prophets appear on the scene with a shocking message: The nation of Israel faces a severe crisis because Yahweh judges all the nations of the world on the basis of whether or not they practice justice. And the test of justice is what happens to the poorest and most marginalized: the orphans, the widows, and the stranger. For Yahweh, the liberation of the poor and oppressed is of greater importance than the survival of any nation or its institutions. In fact, the prophets see themselves called, as Jeremiah put it, "to pluck up and to break down, to destroy and to overthrow, to build and to plant" (1:10). When a wealthy and powerful nation fails to serve the cause of the poor at home and abroad, social stability and international peace can be achieved only through the decline and, if necessary, the defeat of that nation. These prophets were not greatly honored in their time, but their witness was not only preserved but given a central place in the Hebrew Scriptures.

In the New Testament, this way of looking at what is happening in the world is focussed more sharply and stated with even greater intensity. In Jesus of Nazareth, the divine concern for the poor and powerless has assumed human form; *God becomes incarnate in a poor person.* Jesus is born in a stable; his birth is announced to shepherds. He grows up working as a carpenter among the culturally despised of Galilee and declares that his mission is to bring good news to the poor and free them from bondage (Luke 4:16–21).

Moreover, Jesus of Nazareth is declared to be the long-awaited Messiah, the one sent by God to initiate a new era of peace and justice in the world. Jesus himself calls this new order the Reign of God and declares that it belongs to the poor (Luke 6:20). More than this, its establishment represents such a radical transformation of existing structures that the mighty will be brought down and those at the bottom will be raised up; those who are starving will have plenty to eat while the wealthy will be sent away hungry (Luke 1:51–53; 6:20–26).

Jesus lived what he preached, dedicating his energies to healing the sick, empowering the powerless, challenging oppressive structures, both political and religious, at their roots, and bringing together a small nucleus of the poorest and most marginal to form a new community. He also called upon those who wanted to follow him to practice love as they had seen it exemplified in him.

But the most extraordinary element in the life and teaching of Jesus is the sense of urgency he communicates to those around him. This transformation of the world in order to offer new life to the poor and marginal must not be delayed. For Jesus, the decisive event turning the world around has already occurred and a new manifestation of God's Reign is to be expected at any moment. In fact, the yearning for and expectation of the end — as the termination of the present order and the definitive establishment of God's Reign — are so central that the followers of Christ are called to look at the present in the light of its future transformation, and to live and act now *as if* the new day had already dawned. Moreover, in the New Testament, this Jesus of Nazareth is presented as the Savior, the source of abundant life. Those who believe in him are thus led to relate to poor and marginal people as he did, expecting to experience the presence of God and to find a meaningful life as they do so.

All this is so radically different from our customary ways of thinking and acting that we may find it difficult if not impossible to relate it even to our everyday life as persons. And it certainly doesn't provide us with a program for economic or political reform, much less for U.S. policy toward the Third World. But I have found that as I allow this biblical story to break through to me and struggle with it, something much more important happens: it gradually changes my perspective on what is happening around me and awakens new concerns. To the extent that I respond to what the Bible says to me, I find myself living a process of transformation that makes it possible for me to perceive new options for my life and for the future of my country. These, in turn, provide me with useful resources for dealing with specific issues of U.S. policy.

1. This biblical faith has sensitized me to the deprivation and suffering of poor and marginal people as nothing else has done. The richer my experience of God, the closer I find myself drawn to the "wretched of the earth," those to whom everything I cherish has been denied. The more rewarding my relationships with other persons, the greater my anguish over the suffering of the dispossessed. The stronger my hope for the future, the more intense my yearning for their liberation.

One of the persons who best exemplifies this for me is Oscar Romero, the conservative archbishop of San Salvador who gradually was led to take up the cause of the people of his country, and for this was assassinated. Jon Sobrino, one of his colleagues, described his journey. Archbishop Romero, he said,

> living fully in the real world, discovered the most profound truth of this world: the poverty that cries out to heaven. This poverty had the concrete faces of those he loved so much: the children who die; the peasants without land or rights; the inhabitants of the slums; the tortured bodies of village people, whose crime had been their desire to liberate themselves from poverty and oppression.
>
> The poor broke his heart open, and the wound had never healed. The pain of the poor penetrated deeply into his heart. He felt the compassion and mercy of Jesus toward them and made this compassion and mercy the directing principle of all his actions.

2. Sensitivity to the suffering of the "little people" of the world leads to a new awareness of the fact that their suffering has been ignored or downplayed across the centuries even by those who affirm the sacredness of human life. For me as a white, North American male, I find it hard to believe that I and others like me have for so long been oblivious to the pain of Native Americans, of the

victims of slavery and racial discrimination, or of women. I also realize how often we have perceived the pain only of a few close to us and like us, and have used it to distract attention from the suffering we were inflicting on others. Mark Twain called attention to this years ago when he spoke of two "Reigns of Terror":

> There were two "Reigns of Terror,"
> if we would but remember it and consider it;
> the one wrought murder in hot passion,
> the other in heartless cold blood;
> the one lasted mere months,
> the other lasted a thousand years;
> the one inflicted death upon a thousand persons,
> the other upon a hundred millions;
> but our shudders are all for the "horrors"
> of the minor terror, the momentary terror,
> so to speak. (Quoted in Galtung 1980, vii)

3. When these realities become a part of my daily consciousness, the burning question becomes: What can I, my community, and my nation do to overcome this destruction of so many human lives? This changes my perspective on a number of things:

- I perceive that the greatest evil of our time is not Marxism but all that contributes to the suffering and death of the poor before their time. Both Marxism and our own system are to be judged in terms of what they do to maintain the poor in bondage or contribute to their liberation.

- I lose patience with anyone who criticizes those struggling to create a more just society as hopelessly utopian. That too easily limits our options and allows us to live with an intolerable situation. Moreover, in light of the structural violence being maintained today by prevailing economic, political, and social institutions and the fact that our world is hovering on the brink of destruction because of a balance of nuclear power — and terror — the struggle for peace through justice for the poor represents the most realistic approach possible.

- I find myself beginning to look at history as the struggle of the little people of the world for justice and life. They, their yearnings and dreams, their suffering and struggle take on greater significance than the stories of the achievements and heroism, the victories and defeats of the wealthy and powerful. I suspect that my Third World colleagues may be right when they claim that those who suffer, and in their suffering envision and dare to struggle to create a new world, provide the real motive power for history and become its protagonists.

Does it make any sense for us to approach issues of U.S. policy toward the Third World from this perspective? I believe that it does. But before going into it, I want to suggest that this biblical attitude toward the poor has so affected us as a people that we must take it into account if we want to live at peace with ourselves.

## Overcoming a Contradiction in Our Character as a People

When our president reasserts U.S. power over the little nations of the world, we tend to support him enthusiastically. But when we see that such intervention can lead to massive destruction of human life, especially of the innocent poor, we draw back in horror, unable to believe that our country could do such a thing. When our young men take part in such destruction of life, as happened in Vietnam, their lives can be irreparably damaged and the social fabric of our nation is torn apart. We pursue aggressively our individual careers in a drive for wealth and power. And yet, when we are most successful, we are often profoundly dissatisfied and have little hope for the future.

On the other hand, when we take advantage of opportunities to serve others and work for justice, we may derive unusual satisfaction from it. One of the most interesting experiences I had while living in Nicaragua was my contact with North Americans who had gone there to live and work. Most of those I met were not political radicals; for many of them, living and working in Nicaragua — given the climate, the low standard of living, and the inefficiency of the government bureaucracy — was not easy. But they were excited about being there because so many people were working so hard to create a new social order serving the needs of the poor majority and giving them a new place of responsibility in it. Many North Americans I got to know there valued above all else this opportunity to be part of such an enterprise. Since returning to the U.S.A., I have been surprised by the number of women and men I have met who have expressed a longing to be involved in something similar at home or abroad.

Why do we, in our affluence, yearn for this and get upset when we realize that our nation is involved — directly or indirectly — in the death of people in Third World countries? I'm convinced that a partial answer is to be found in our national character as it has developed over generations.

Many of the early settlers who came here from Europe were fleeing from religious persecution or political tyranny. Others were so poor that they were willing to cut their ties with family and homeland, risk a long and dangerous sea voyage, and face the untamed wilderness, in order to have an opportunity to begin again. Gradually, the poor and oppressed in many lands came to look on the United States as the one place in the world where they could hope to find shelter and freedom, as well as a chance for a decent human life. In 1780, T. Pownall, a British gentleman, declared that the United States of America "will become a Nation to whom all nations will come, a People to whom the Remnants of all ruined people will fly, whom all the oppressed and injured of every nation will seek for refuge" (quoted in Rosenstock-Huessy 1964, 675). This vision of America has been passed on from one generation to another and has become an integral part of our self-identity as a people.

In our dealings with Native Americans, blacks, and other minorities, we have failed to live up to this vision. But that does not alter the fact that, as a people, we are committed to certain values on which our nation was founded: opportunity for all, social justice, and freedom for the human spirit to dream of a new future and struggle to create it. What ultimately matters to us is to be engaged in the transformation of our nation in line with this vision and in the defense of these values abroad. When we depart from this path, we lose our soul and our national life disintegrates. As Walter Lippman once remarked, our conscience is a reality, and we cannot move ahead if we abandon our own principles in defense of our nation.

To the extent that one generation after another of North Americans have been influenced by the biblical heritage to which we have referred above, and have succeeded in passing it on to us, we will be able to feel at home here only if we sense that our nation is moving toward this goal at home and abroad. In fact, we will be hopeful about the future of our country only when we are convinced that our tremendous economic resources and our power are contributing to the liberation of the poor and oppressed peoples of the world.

For us today, that does not mean primarily welcoming them to these shores and giving them a new chance here but rather doing what we can as a nation to support their efforts to transform their own countries into lands of opportunity for the common people. It means, in other words, that we support the struggles of the little nations of the world to achieve today what we fought a war to achieve two hundred years ago. At the heart of our democratic ideal is the conviction that justice and stability are possible only when those at the bottom have a chance to express their needs in the political process. Fair representation is the key to avoiding tyranny, whether it be by a king or a military dictator, by a distant parliament imposing an unwanted tax on tea or a powerful nation imposing its own political and economic order on small countries. Democracy means recognizing and honoring the right of poor countries to decide how best to use their limited economic resources to meet the needs of their own people rather than to be the victims of economic exploitation by powerful international interests.

By living out our ideal of a society of opportunity for those formerly denied a chance, we have helped create new expectations and have inspired poor nations to organize their economic life around meeting the needs of the majority. As a nation, we have so exalted the democratic ideal, by our words and our example, that we have encouraged popular movements in the Third World that go beyond our representative democracy in their efforts to make it possible for those at the bottom to participate in the exercise of public power.

Unfortunately, some of the scholars and diplomats who play a major role in shaping our policy not only back off from the implications of this heritage but come up with all sorts of reasons for doing so. Harvard professor Samuel P. Huntington is one of them. In *The Crisis of Democracy,* he recognizes the dramatic renewal of the democratic spirit that occurred in this country in the 1960s, expressed in a renewed commitment to the idea of equality, increased concern for the rights and opportunities of minorities and women, and a pervasive criticism of those who possessed excessive power and wealth. He even goes so far as to declare that "the roots of the surge are to be found in the basic American value system and the degree of commitment that groups in society feel toward that value system" (Crozier, Huntington, Joji 1975, 112). But then, instead of affirming this as the foundation for a new adventure in the development of our political institutions as well as in our relations with Third World countries, he speaks of it as a crisis. This crisis, according to Huntington, is producing a breakdown of authority, the loss of the compulsion to obey those previously considered superior, and the general weakening of confidence in institutions and their leaders. In this situation, he focuses attention on the limits to the extension of political democracy and ends up providing a rationale for U.S. support of governments that "restrict democracy." Third World leaders struggling to create authentic democratic institutions, who may have been inspired by our Declaration of Independence and our democratic institutions, will be more inclined to see this as evidence that we are deceiving ourselves and becoming the enemies of the poor people of the world. We should hardly be surprised if they become more disillusioned with us and turn elsewhere for inspiration and guidance.

If our religious faith helps us escape from this ideological bind, we may be able to perceive the alternative open to us: to be led by our heritage to think and act *globally*. Given the fact that we now all live in one "global village," in close contact with each other, and are increasingly interdependent, we can serve our national self-interest only as we take into account the interests of all nations. As Richard Barnet has put it, "In order to develop the strength to act in the world so that our children and grandchildren may live we will have to rebuild our faith in the possibilities of a decent society — not just for ourselves but for our four billion neighbors" (1981, 118).

# Chapter 4

# HUMAN WELL-BEING AND
# THE NATIONAL INTEREST

BIBLICAL FAITH COMPELS US to raise constantly the question of how our policies affect the people of the Third World and to insist that our government, in working out its relations with them, give central importance to their well-being. This not only calls for a fundamental change in attitude but also leaves us with a problem for which there is no easy answer: How can we as a nation contribute significantly to economic development serving the interests of the poor majority around the world and at the same time defend the legitimate interests of our own people? The answer to this question can come only as a result of long-term study and analysis, dialogue with a new generation of leaders in the developing countries, and a great deal of trial and error as we try out new policies and learn from our experience.

The problem is difficult, but answers to it can be found if we are willing to face the realities of a new historical era. In fact, I would argue that, because of our bondage to outmoded perspectives, we have missed many opportunities to support efforts of Third World peoples to improve their lot that might at the same time contribute to rather than work against our national self-interest. For some of the policies we now pursue end up laying unnecessarily heavy burdens upon us, while alternatives that might benefit us as well as our poor neighbors remain largely unexplored. Here I want to call attention to four areas in which concern for the poor of the world could lead to changes that might reduce rather than increase

43

our burden as a nation and allow us to play a more positive role in the creation of a new international order.

## The Cost of Oppression

*Our present policy of supporting a small ruling class that uses its power to exploit and repress the people is becoming more and more costly for us.*

A small percentage of the money we provide to these ruling groups ever reaches the poor or goes toward economic development. Much of it is used by them to increase their wealth and augment their private accounts in foreign banks. We are supporting those who are robbing us and their own people. The Somoza family in Nicaragua used U.S. aid and even money sent to help the victims of the 1972 earthquake to build up a fortune of hundreds of millions of dollars, much of it invested abroad. More recently, we have been scandalized by similar disclosures regarding the Marcos family in the Philippines. Over a period of two years, 1982 and 1983, when the U.S.A. was pouring hundreds of millions of dollars into El Salvador, a few ruling families and military officers allied with them put an estimated one billion dollars into their private accounts abroad.

Moreover, this wealthy elite is primarily interested in making and spending money and using their power to preserve what they have, not to create a new economic order serving the needs of the people. The deprivation and suffering of the masses is of little concern to them. Even when one-third or more of the population is unemployed or underemployed, when social unrest mounts and it is clear to anyone with eyes to see that the traditional economic structures are no longer functioning, these elites lack the vision and the will to seek and find solutions to the problems before them.

This is evident, for example, in Brazil where a military government made use of large loans from U.S. banks to build highways and dams and stimulate economic development. But after twenty years of this type of development under military rule, inflation reached 250 percent, 68 percent of the population was undernourished, and the situation of the urban and rural poor was more desperate than before.

In 1983, I visited El Salvador as a member of a delegation made up of two members of Congress and women and men representing the world of business and labor, the university and the church. We spent a great deal of time with those in positions of power in the government, in the military, and in private circles. What most shocked us was to see how unconcerned these leaders were about what we perceived to be overwhelming economic and social problems.

Under these circumstances, the U.S.A. may want to see major reforms; these elites at best do little to create conditions under which such reforms can succeed; at worst, they sabotage them. We talk about more equitable economic development and democracy; they are concerned to keep what they have. Sooner or later, they are forced to rely more and more on violence and repression to keep the poor under control and abandon even the pretense of defending human rights or preserving democracy. As the suffering of the masses increases and their protests grow, these ruling elites become even more dependent on the U.S.A. for military as well as economic aid. The longer we support them in their efforts to preserve rather than transform their societies, the greater the economic burden we assume and the more we are discredited among those who find the status quo intolerable.

On the other hand, *U.S. support for governments attempting to break the domination of a small and wealthy ruling class, broaden the base of participation in public life, and improve the lot of the masses could make it possible for us to do much more than we are now doing to help overcome the scourge of poverty.*

Government officials in Washington frequently declare that our country will be flooded with refugees if the Sandinistas continue in power in Nicaragua and revolutionary movements triumph elsewhere. This may play on our fears, but it has little to do with reality. The vast majority of poor people from south of our border who are now pounding on our doors are not from Nicaragua, but from countries like El Salvador and Guatemala that not only keep their people in conditions of extreme poverty but use violence against those who want to bring about change. Hunger, unemployment, and the forcing of peasants off the land, coupled with political repression, create refugees; the flow of people northward will slow down only when movements committed to improving the lot of the poor take power and create a new economic and political order.

We North Americans don't want to see Third World people starve or continue to live in miserable conditions. We want their situation to change. But we are often quite naive when it comes to understanding how this can happen. It will not happen by the U.S. trying to impose its economic and political system; it cannot come about by our pressing the ruling elites to bring about reforms or providing them with large amounts of money. The poor majority will have a better life only as committed groups of men and women in each country have the opportunity to find the right solutions for their situation and to work night and day over many years to construct a new society.

One of the reasons why many North Americans who travel to Nicaragua return with a positive attitude toward that country is that they have seen this sacrificial outpouring of life by women and men committed to offering a new life of opportunity to the poor. On my first visit there after the victory of the revolution, this is what most caught my attention. As a result of living and traveling in Central and South America over many years, I had come to realize that poverty could be overcome, if at all, only by an almost superhuman effort of the part of large numbers of people throughout society. In Nicaragua, I saw this happening. I met individuals and teams in the ministries of housing and education and the program of land reform who had a clear vision of what they could do to serve the people, were committed to it, and were working very hard on low salaries to achieve their goals. They were joined by many others in intermediate positions and at the grassroots who were equally committed to building a new society as they participated, often as volunteers, in programs of adult education, preventive medicine and health care, the development of farm cooperatives, etc. The bureaucracy often functioned inefficiently and the number of people with this sense of dedication was all too small. But for the first time in my life, I saw people throughout society working energetically to create a social order serving the interests of the poor and getting results even under the most adverse circumstances.

Those who engage in this task will not be inclined to take orders from the U.S. embassy, support us uncritically in international assemblies, or accept policies affecting them that are made unilaterally by us. In the beginning, they may be very critical of us and their rhetoric may be harsh. But they know that they need U.S. support and economic help; most of them also want to work out positive relationships with us. I'm convinced, moreover, that most of those who are Marxists have international nonalignment as their goal, not subordination to another superpower. They know that their national self-interest will not be served if they become a pawn in the hands of the Soviet Union or get involved in the East-West struggle. The goals they have set for economic and political development can be realized only as they cultivate favorable relations of interdependence with other countries in the region and cordial relations with the United States.

A Christian conscience, sensitive to the needs of the poor and aware of the struggles going on around the world to change their situation, will be aware of the opportunities our nation has to support and participate in these efforts and will press our government to take advantage of them. We will denounce as irrational and counterproductive the tendency to declare that any regime committed to providing food, housing, basic education, and medical care for all must be our enemy while accepting as our friend almost any repressive regime exercising power on behalf of a few landowners and industrialists.

## Advantages of Solidarity

*As the poor people become more aware of their situation and participate more actively in popular organizations struggling to change it, any policy on our part that opposes these developments will contribute to the political instability and violent social upheavals we most fear. Sympathetic understanding and support of such movements could contribute significantly to the struggle against poverty and lead to a new era in U.S.A.–Third World relations.*

In a number of Third World countries, people's movements of one sort or another have arisen from time to time across the centuries. Today, the proliferation of popular organizations among the poorest, in rural and urban areas, goes on at a new pace and represents a major new force in the political arena. Those who have been most marginal and powerless are coming together more or less spontaneously to find solutions to their most urgent problems and make their voices heard. As they organize soup kitchens, provide child care for each other, or demand health care and jobs from public officials, they discover their own worth as human beings as well as their ability to act to bring about change. Distrustful of traditional political leaders and parties, they nevertheless know that they must act politically and negotiate with them. Especially in Latin America, the Christian base communities have been a major factor in the development of these movements and in the formation of their leaders.

In Nicaragua, these movements played a major role in the popular insurrection that overthrew the Somoza dictatorship; since the triumph of the revolution, the Sandinistas have encouraged such popular participation in national reconstruction as well as the continuation of the small Christian communities among the peasants and the urban poor. Where these movements are strong, the revolution comes closer to achieving its goals in the areas of public health, adult education, agricultural production, etc. At the same time, people formerly excluded from national life are becoming active participants in the political process. In El Salvador, popular organizations of peasants and industrial workers, teachers and students, have become such a threat to the ruling oligarchy that they have been massively suppressed in recent years: more than 40,000 men, women, and children were killed largely by "uniformed men" and death squads from 1981 to 1985. And the fact that such movements continue to spring up and grow under conditions of extreme repression witnesses to their vitality.

These popular movements are not only here to stay; they are going to play an increasingly important role in the political development of Third World countries over the next decades. The success or failure of U.S. policy will depend to no small degree upon our ability to understand what they represent and recognize the potential they hold for laying the foundation for a new type of economic development and participatory democracy.

This is something our own history as a people should prepare us to understand and support. From the beginning, we have seen ourselves as a nation in which "the common man" has had a unique place and opportunity. We North Americans speak proudly of ourselves as having a free society in which no class rules, elites are not so entrenched, and the little people have not only a place but wide-open doors to opportunity. We still have a long way to go to attain this goal. But the fact remains that it is an essential part of our national self-understanding. Today, the emergence of people's movements in the Third World challenges us to recover that part of our heritage and to live it out in our relations with the little nations of the world.

Unfortunately, there are other forces in our society that are pulling us in the opposite direction. We may be descendants of poor immigrants who made it, but that does not necessarily mean that we are committed to providing such opportunities for the poor and marginal today. In the last few years, a new elitist paternalism seems to be more in vogue. George Gilder in his book, *Wealth and Poverty,* popular for a time with members of the Reagan administration, states clearly: "Democratic masses cannot be generative or creative, they can merely react and ratify." "Representative democracy is a better system than any other chiefly because it evokes the experimental competition of elites" (p. 38). And Eileen Gardner, appointed as a policy consultant for the Department of Education in Washington (and later forced to resign), wrote, in a report to the Heritage Foundation, that federal funding for the poor and handicapped was "counterproductive": "Man cannot...within one short life span...raise the lower to meet the higher." "The only way the performance of the lower can be made equal to that of the higher is artificially to constrain and pervert the performance of the higher" (*The Philadelphia Inquirer,* April 17, 1985).

Such claims may sound shocking to our ears, but they only express, in strident language, something that has been asserted again and again by the elite of our Western societies. Thomas Carlyle claimed that universal history was, at bottom, the history of the great men who have worked here. And when the political scientist Carl Friedrich carried on a historical investigation of the place of the "common man" in Europe and North America, he came to this conclusion:

When we look over the field of political writings of the last hundred years, we find a veritable avalanche of writers extolling the virtues of the few who are wise, if not virtuous, as contrasted with the low-brow belief in the common man.... The history of antidemocratic elite doctrines is a dominant theme in the history of Western thought in the last three generations. (1942, 245–246)

Christian sensitivity to the needs and capacities of the "common people" of the world can change our perception and perspective and open our eyes to a number of things:

- The tendency of the wealthy and powerful to extol beyond reason their own virtues and abilities to govern, and to exaggerate the political limitations of the poor, at the same time that they deny them the opportunity to participate more in public life and learn from experience.

- The failure of the elite to recognize how poor a job they have done in ordering the world. To get some sense of this, we need only call to mind the possibility we face of a nuclear holocaust, the problems we have with pollution, the absurd situation in which millions are dying of hunger while we are urged daily to consume more in order to keep the system going, or the absurd rationalizations those in power come up with to justify their destructive acts.

- The extent to which the growing obsession in some quarters with law, order, and national security is an outgrowth of the fear taking hold of the elite as others demand a more significant role in society. The emergence of new groups and classes in society calls for the transformation of our major institutions; the tendency of those in power — whether in Western liberal or in Marxist societies — is to react out of fear of loss, by reaffirming the value of old structures and finding new means of keeping the people at the bottom under control.

- The possibility that the poor majority may be as well or better prepared than the elite to act politically: Their thought about society is a product of living and struggling together, not just the reflection of independent individuals. It may be more organic, more in touch with their day-to-day realities, more closely related to their culture and traditions and less dominated by compartmentalized bureaucratic categories. Above all, the common people are better prepared to know what is good for them than is any elite.

- The possibility that in situations where economic and social problems can be solved only as new structures are developed, the victims of the established order are more likely to have the vision and the will necessary for that task than are those who benefit from the status quo. They likewise are the ones who can provide a political base for bringing about the changes we say we favor.

If we as a nation are willing to re-examine our democratic heritage in the light of the new popular movements emerging in the Third World, we will realize that these movements provide the foundation for new experiments in democracy that may turn out to be very much in line with our own ideals. The United States has a historic opportunity to support them and those associated with them in their struggle against antidemocratic forces, whether they be members of the ruling elite, doctrinaire Marxists, or others. As we do this, the poor people of the world may look to us once again as their allies in the struggle for a decent human life.

## The Path to Economic Independence

*Exploitation of Third World countries weakens them economically and makes them more dependent. When we encourage them to follow their own road to economic development, using their resources to meet the needs of the people, we help to strengthen them economically and thus to become less dependent on us.*

We don't have to be experts in economic matters to realize that when we deny other countries the right to be in charge of their own economic life, something we as a nation fought a war to achieve, the result will be disastrous. If our economic power creates a situation in which the development of a poor country is oriented around our priorities rather than theirs, they will be less able to produce what the people most need. This can result in widespread malnutrition and starvation. When foreign interests control the mining and refining of minerals and the production of other items for export, poor nations are deprived of resources they would otherwise have for meeting the needs of their people. This is especially true when the industrialized nations set the prices for what they import as well as other terms of trade. Economic development in line with our priorities focuses attention on the production and purchase of things within the reach of only a small percentage of the population. Only those who have salaries many times higher than the majority of people can benefit from that system. Moreover, once this small elite group gets caught up in consumerism, they will not be greatly concerned about a type of economic development that is oriented toward meeting the basic needs of the majority of the people. They are more likely to be among the first to denounce as "Communist" any attempt to move in this direction.

Economic development in poor countries can bring social stability and peace only as they have control of their own resources as well as a larger say in setting prices for their exports and other terms of trade. It calls for increased trade and economic cooperation in each region and with other peripheral countries, rather than the continuation of bilateral relations of the colonial type. And such developments will come about only as a new generation of men and women, oriented toward the people and identified with their struggle, are able to imagine and create new economic models.

The time has come for Third World nations, especially the smaller and poorer ones, to find their own way and solve their own problems. In doing this, they may come up with patterns of economic life that are quite different from the patterns found in the U.S.A. and other Western industrial countries as well as in the Soviet bloc. As regards future relations between Third World and industrialized nations, there is an urgent need for a New International Economic Order, something that the U.S.A. should support vigorously as an essential step toward a more stable and more peaceful world.

All this raises fundamental questions about the future of transnational corporations in Third World countries, questions which cannot be explored here in any depth. But in line with what we have said thus far, one thing should be clear: To the extent that a religious concern for the poor people of the world comes to the fore, these corporations will be judged on the basis of their ability — or inability — to contribute to the type of economic development outlined here. Most of us in the U.S.A. have not gone very far in envisioning what this might mean. But a new generation of Christians in Asia, Africa, and Latin America, who are committed to a type of economic development serving the needs of the people, have given a great deal of thought to this matter, and we would be wise to listen to what they have to say. On the one hand, they are sharply critical of the impact transnational corporations are now having in their countries. An *Asia Region Working Paper*, prepared for a recent ecumenical conference, declares:

The transnational corporate system distorts our national and local economies by creating structural bifurcation between rural and industrial sectors of the economy, by concentrating ownership of the capital and land, by making the people and their economy totally dependent upon a worldwide market system, by exploiting the cheap labor market, by draining financial resources and by exploiting natural resources.

On the other hand, they are suggesting that the transnationals can contribute to national economic development if they honor what a particular country is doing to set its own terms economically, and are willing to work more closely with those involved in this process as they decide what they will do and how they will function. In fact, in situations in which the economic development of a country is in the hands of its own people and serves their interests, these corporations may find that they can make a significant contribution to the well-being of the people as a whole.

In this area of economic relations, there are no easy answers. But we can be engaged in thinking up and testing out alternatives rather than defending obsolete patterns of relationship that work against the people, and eventually against us as well. Changes in the direction suggested here could mean, in some cases, an economic loss for the U.S.A. But given our wealth, our technological development, and the power of our economy, we should not be too disturbed by changes which would allow poor nations to develop their own resources or organize their economy to serve their interests. If we have to exploit the poorest people of the world in order to keep our economy functioning efficiently, then we should raise serious questions about our own economic system.

## The Specter of Marxism

*When the U.S.A. opposes any regime that takes up the cause of the poor majority because it is or might become Marxist, we abandon our own vision of who we are as a nation and are perceived by many in the Third World as the enemy of the poor. If we support those movements struggling for justice for the poor, we will be challenged to expand our vision of who we are and explore new options in international relations.*

The threat that international Communism presents to the peace of the world, plus the antidemocratic nature of Communist regimes in Eastern Europe and elsewhere, make us justifiably apprehensive about the role Marxism plays in Third World countries. But if we become so obsessed with this concern that we ignore the suffering of the poor and overlook the failure of our own society to achieve justice and participatory democracy, we develop a very distorted picture of the situation. And our fear of losing something may make it easy for us to become victims of those who use this fear as a weapon to preserve the status quo, at home and abroad, at all costs.

It is at this point that a vital Christian faith enables us to overcome our fear and see what is happening from a different perspective. Our commitment to the poor and their struggle is so compelling that the presence of Marxists in the same struggle cannot become an excuse for us to abandon it. Our faith awakens in us a passion for justice and strengthens our conviction that God is acting in the world to create a new order serving the interests of those now suffering and exploited, and that we have a responsibility to struggle for it.

In this context, we can look honestly at what is happening in Third world nations, the role Marxism is really playing, and how our fear of Communism is being exploited. When we do this, a number of things stand out:

- Governments that are committed to the economic and political emancipation of the common people have been attacked as Communist in order to justify U.S. involvement in efforts to overthrow them. The result has often been greater suffering for the poor majority, social instability, and brutal repression — leading almost inevitably to the emergence of more radical movements for change.

    We referred earlier to the overthrow of the moderately progressive Arbenz regime in Guatemala in 1954 and the fate of the democratically elected regime of Salvador Allende in Chile in 1973. Now the Reagan administration has denounced Nicaragua as a "totalitarian dungeon," and the CIA is providing economic and military support for counterrevolutionary guerrillas on its borders. Once again, we appear as the enemies of a revolution that is attempting to structure the economy around the needs of the poor majority while encouraging greater political participation at all levels of national life. The *contras* we support, on the other hand, have little political support within the country, have shown no desire to improve the lot of the poor, and are militarily controlled by leaders of the Somozan National Guard, whose brutality and lack of concern for the people brought on a popular insurrection.

- Marxism is branded as a monolithic party, dominated by a rigid ideological orthodoxy. Any movement in which Marxists play a major role is assumed to fit this stereotype at the very moment when reality increasingly defies it, especially in the Third World. In a number of countries, there are various parties and movements committed to revolutionary change, with differing ideologies and degrees of Marxist influence. Often those that are most rigid and most closely tied to international Communism are least effective and frequently marginalized. The movements closest to the people and their struggles tend to be less interested in abstract philosophical doctrines, more oriented toward the culture and history of their own people, and engaged in a search for authentic solutions to their own problems. And in Latin America and elsewhere, the increasing participation of Christians in movements for change on their own terms adds another dimension to the ideological picture.

- Our government, while harshly attacking "international Communism," is strangely inconsistent in its pattern of relationships with Marxist regimes. We refuse to give economic aid to Nicaragua, a country about which the Soviet Union has serious doubts as to whether it can be considered socialist, and we urge other governments and international funding agencies to do the same. But we provide economic assistance to Eastern European countries that are rigidly Marxist and within the Soviet orbit. We are involved in efforts to overthrow the Nicaraguan government, accusing it of threatening to intervene in other countries in the region when it is struggling desperately for survival, while having favorable relations with China, which has intervened in Vietnam. We are providing military support to the Marxist Khmer Rouge in Cambodia — which while in power killed millions — against another Marxist regime that has at least brought more security to its people. And we denounce Nicaragua, which recently held a free election open to a range of opposition parties, as "totalitarian" and a threat to democracy, while supporting rightist dictatorships which kill political opponents, threaten opposition movements, and hold fake elections, or China, which doesn't even predict when it will hold elections. For anyone who looks honestly at this picture, it is difficult to avoid the conclusion that our anti-Communism is all too often a weapon used to block the type of social change that could improve the life of the dispossessed people in the Third World.

In Latin America, and elsewhere in the Third World, Christians with a passion for justice have become fully involved in struggles for change. In their inescapable encounter with Marxists, their attitude toward Marxism has been transformed as they in turn are transforming the struggles in which they are engaged. Their experience may have something to say to us in the U.S.A.

Their first surprise is often the discovery that many of the Marxists they meet are people like themselves who can no longer stand idly by in the face of so much poverty, suffering, and death around them; men and women for whom Marxism had provided a vision of a new and more just society, tools for analysis of the present order, and ways of working to overcome it. Often young men and women influenced by Marxism turn out to be the only other people Christians can find who are not primarily interested in pursuing their own private careers, making money as they move upward and enjoying the benefits offered to a few in the new consumer society. In fact, young Marxists often have a sense of commitment to the cause of the poor and a willingness to give their lives to it that puts to shame Christians for whom such a spirit of dedication would seem to be the most natural outgrowth of their faith.

Christians who participate in movements for radical change find that some of their Marxist companions rigidly adhere to the dogma of dialectical materialism, which provides them with all the answers. In any organization in which that dogmatic mentality is dominant, the participation of Christians will be extremely difficult, if not impossible.

We in the United States tend to think that all Marxists and Marxist movements are of this type; Christians in Latin America are discovering that this is not the case. Marxism, to be sure, has its "fundamentalists," and Marxist movements in Europe and North America have often shown a propensity to dogmatism possessing, as they do, a system of thought claiming to be the truth. But some Marxist movements in Third World countries have developed in a quite different way. They include, among their members, many peasants and poor urban folk. As these men and women come to understand why they are poor and how their society can be changed, they may speak about oppression, class struggle, social justice, and socialism. But they have little or no interest in "dialectical materialism" or the rational conceptualization that goes with it. Their intellectual and spiritual world remains that of their religious and cultural heritage, and their motivation for the struggle for justice comes from it. Many of a new generation of university students and professionals, who live in solidarity with the poor and come to know better their culture and history, develop their own "criollo" Marxism as well. As I have observed during my travels in recent years, these women and men, if they can be called Marxists, are primarily *humanists,* in the sense that they are primarily interested in the liberation of suffering people and the creation of a more human society, not in endless discussions of theory and philosophy.

There is, of course, no guarantee that Third World Marxist movements will evolve in this direction in the future. In countries where those struggling for justice are most persecuted, those following a more rigid ideological line may win out, at least for a time. But even in those situations, two factors work in the opposite direction. The proliferation of popular organizations in rural and urban areas, and the new sense of subjecthood that is growing among their members, mean that these popular movements will resist such dogmatism. Some Marxists leaders who are in contact with these movements have been influenced by these developments and are committed to encouraging such participation and developing political and social institutions that restructure power from the bottom up. Moreover, the presence of increasing numbers of Christians who have a solid theological foundation and are living the experience of the base communities creates a new situation which challenges Marxism to be more faithful to its own humanistic vision.

The major question to be raised about the future of these revolutionary movements is not whether or not they are Marxist, whatever that may mean today. It is rather: *Can those involved in this struggle, Marxists, Christians, and others, keep alive their fundamental commitment to the poor, and struggle to create a new society that offers them increasing participation, economically and in the exercise of power?*

These developments confront us with a new challenge. We cannot meet it by using stereotypes that no longer apply. Only as we learn to discern what is happening in each situation and make an honest assessment of the potential present in it for creative response to the cry of the poor will we be able to play a positive role in the future.

# Chapter 5

# UTOPIAN VISION:
# IN THE BIBLE AND THE THIRD WORLD

WHILE MANY U.S. CITIZENS are becoming increasingly apprehensive about the future role of their country in the world of nations and are obsessed with the preservation of the position we now hold, a small but significant community of those oriented by religious faith are beginning to imagine a new future for the U.S.A. As they have gone to Nicaragua and elsewhere in Central America with Witness for Peace or other groups, their contact with people attempting to build a more just society has led them to dream of a new place for our nation as it supports such struggles. Those living in close contact with refugees from El Salvador and Guatemala in the Sanctuary movement have come to a similar vision as they have gotten close to the suffering of uprooted people in that region and become aware of the hope they have for a better life. As this new breed of Christians gather in small groups to study what is happening there and examine present U.S. policy, they become aware of alternatives that have not been explored and think of the United States as a nation capable of envisioning and working to create a new international order.

Not surprisingly, the Bible is making a major contribution to this change in outlook. Many of us are discovering, as we read it once again, that this book focuses our attention not so much on what has already been achieved, great as it may be, but on the *unfulfilled possibilities in and beyond the present moment*. That which already exists is seen in the light of what it can become. The yearning for a better future is stronger than the desire for the security that comes from hanging on to what one already has. In fact, the dreamed-of future, which is seen as already breaking into the present, sets the terms for what we do and think now.

This revolution in historical perception is the result of a profound change in the understanding of the nature of God that occurred among the people of Israel. Their God, Yahweh, constantly present in their midst, is the One who goes ahead of them. When Moses inquires about the name of this God, Yahweh replies, "I will be who I will be" (Exod. 3:14). The closer the Israelites get to this God, the more intense is their yearning for a future in which human life and history will reach a new level of fulfillment.

## God's Promised Reign

In an earlier chapter, we looked at certain central events in biblical history in which God's concern for the poor was disclosed. In each of them, we also find this orientation toward a new and promising future:

1. The Exodus from Egypt, so central in the Old Testament, is only the beginning of a long journey toward a *promised land,* a land "flowing with milk and honey." The gods of the great empires supported their rulers as they struggled to build up their power and expand their conquests to include more people over whom they could rule and whom they might exploit. But Yahweh is the God of a small group of slaves in Egypt, not of the pharaoh. This God calls them to leave Egypt in order to create a new social order and thus change the course of history.

While the great empires, occupying center stage, are going about their usual business, this band of slaves who escaped from Egypt spend forty years wandering in the desert, in poverty and complete insecurity. During that time, they slowly learn how to organize their life in a new way. Yahweh directs them to develop their economy along essentially egalitarian lines and overcome the oppressiveness of hierarchical structures through the diffusion of power throughout society. Special attention is to be given to those who are marginal socially and economically: the widow, the orphan, and the stranger. In addition, they are commanded by Yahweh to observe every fiftieth year as a Year of Jubilee, during which debts are to be cancelled, slaves set free, and the land redistributed.

Slaves, who had possessed nothing of their own, lived by the promise that they would someday own land; those who had been viciously exploited dreamed of a land flowing with milk and honey. But the struggle was long and arduous. When the Israelites at last established themselves in Canaan, what they were able to accomplish fell far short of their dreams. Time and again, the people yearned for their past life and were tempted to abandon their vision of the future. Their thoughts turned to the "fleshpots of Egypt," and they declared that they would rather have died in the oppressive situation they knew than face the unknown and struggle to create something that did not exist. Rather make their own idols who would guarantee what they already had and leave them in peace than continue to worship Yahweh who was always driving them toward the unknown.

From the time of Moses onward, a few men and women in each generation kept the dream alive, even when Yahweh's experiment seemed to have failed completely. But whatever the immediate results, a new way of looking at life and history — and of relating to God — had been introduced into the world and established as the norm for a community of faith. At the center of the Jewish and Christian traditions, faith in God has, from this time forward, been identified with the movement of history toward a new and more promising future. Or, as Michael Walzer puts it in his study of the Exodus, to the extent that these memories shape our perception, "wherever you live, it is probably Egypt," but "there is a better place, a world more attractive, a promised land" (Walzer 1985, 149).

2. Several centuries after the people of Israel had established themselves in Canaan, it was all too clear that the dreamed-of future had not come and was not around the corner. The prophets responded to that situation by analyzing what was happening from the perspective of an even more utopian vision.

As society moved from one crisis to another, the situation was not one to inspire hope. Corruption throughout society, oppression and exploitation of the poor similar to that experienced by the Israelites in Egypt, internal political divisions, and repeated invasions or threats of invasion from foreign armies: these constituted the harsh realities of everyday life. For a people who firmly believed that their God had chosen them to live as a nation in such a way that they would be a "light" to the whole world, these developments could only bring disorientation and a profound crisis of meaning.

Some responded by claiming that all was going well, in spite of the evidence to the contrary. Others admitted that the situation was critical but claimed that the God who had done such great things in their favor in the past would certainly protect them, especially if they were more faithful in their religious observances. Still others came to the conclusion that their God had let them down and turned to other gods for help.

The prophets took another approach to the situation. In line with the Exodus/Promised Land tradition, their faith in Yahweh led them to envision a future that went far beyond anything previously dreamed of. Moses had laid before his people a vision of a promised land; the prophets speak of a *new Israel* and a *new Jerusalem*, a society so transformed that "all the nations shall flow to it," finding there a model to guide them (Isa. 2:2, 3). That future will bring with it the end of conquest by foreign powers as well as the end of oppression of the poor at home. Every yoke will be broken and each inhabitant of the land will be able to sit under his or her own vine and fig tree, "and none shall make them afraid" (Micah 4:4).

Jeremiah, usually thought of as the most pessimistic of them all, goes even further and speaks of a more fundamental change: God will make a new covenant and the Law will be written on the hearts of the people.

For some of the prophets, this new age will be established by a *Messiah*, a special person sent by God to bring deliverance. Some refer to him as a great political leader, a new King David; elsewhere a small remnant gathered from the humble and despised is declared to be the bearer of it, and in Deutero-Isaiah we find the rich imagery of the *Suffering Servant*. But in and through all of these, two things are repeatedly affirmed: a profound belief in a new future and the conviction that it will become a reality because God can be trusted to usher it in.

In religious and political circles today this element in the thinking of the Old Testament prophets is often viewed quite negatively. Visions of a new society are denounced as "utopian" and therefore unrealistic, and anything associated with the word "messianic" is thought to lead inevitably to fanaticism. But the historic achievement of the prophets was to make it possible for men and women in decaying societies to transform the dead end in which they were caught into a new beginning, and to affirm that new principles of social, economic, and political organization can be not only thought but also established in history.

3. Jesus situated himself directly in the Exodus/prophetic line, not only by reaffirming this future orientation but also by spelling out, in the most radical way, what it means to allow the future to set the terms for life in the present. With tremendous confidence in the presence and action, in history, of a God who is *creating a new heaven and a new earth,* Jesus added new dimensions to this perception of what is going on in history and challenged those who believe in this God to live this future now with an unusual sense of urgency.

Jesus announced the advent of God's Reign, belonging to the poor, in which those who are hungry will be satisfied, and those who suffer because of material need, rejection, oppression, blindness, or sickness will suffer no more. It is this fundamentally utopian vision of the Reign of God that is at the heart of Jesus' teaching and influences directly his response to every situation.

Moreover, Jesus declared that this future is already present in his person. In a situation in which people were longing desperately for deliverance from bondage and were dreaming of a new messianic age, Jesus allowed his disciples to speak of him as the Messiah. But he also made it perfectly clear that this meant the beginning of a new era. When John the Baptist sent his disciples to inquire of Jesus whether he was the one "who is to come," Jesus replied that "the blind receive their sight, the lame walk, lepers are cleansed, and the deaf hear, the dead are raised up, the poor have good news preached to them" (Luke 7:22). The future envisioned is not a concept or a blueprint; it is a reality incarnate in a person, taking shape in and through his actions and the community around him.

For Jesus, the Reign of God is already breaking into the present; the dreamed-of future is even now taking shape; the restructuring of society for the benefit of those at the bottom is happening. This is the reason why he has Good News for the poor. This is the reason why he speaks of God's Reign as a pearl of great price or a treasure hidden in a field, for the purchase of which one will sell everything one owns. And from this perspective, the ethical teachings of Jesus make sense. If the new order of God's Reign is being created here and now, then anyone who believes this news has no choice but to live in accordance with that reality — loving the enemy, turning the other cheek, sharing with those in need. For only by moving in this direction and living according to a new set of rules can Jesus' disciples participate in the creation of something new.

At the same time, every new order will stand under judgment. God's Reign will not be fully present in any revolution. The Christ (Messiah) who has come will come again, and only then will all things be transformed. Thus, all attempts to build a new order must be open to further transformation in the light of what could be.

4. On first contact, the Apostle Paul seems to belong to another world of thought. He says nothing about the Reign of God and gives little attention to the life and words of Jesus of Nazareth. But we soon discover that his thought is also oriented toward the future; as a matter of fact, in his letters we have the most radical eschatological approach in the New Testament. Paul asks his readers to focus their attention on a new world, a "new age" as he calls it, and challenges them to look at all of life and history from this vantage point. Moreover, Jesus the Messiah is at the center of all this as the object of faith.

Professor J. Christiaan Beker, in his book *Paul the Apostle,* claims that we can understand the thought of Paul, especially this dimension of it, only if we take into account his close association with the Jewish apocalyptic thought of his time. After living in subjection to foreign powers for six centuries, the Jewish people desperately yearned for liberation from bondage and hoped for a Messiah who would bring it about. In the apocalyptic movements, all this was sharply accentuated. They spoke of the most radical discrepancy between what is and what could be, the "present evil age," as Paul called it, and the "age to come." They longed for and expected the direct intervention of God in history to liberate not only Israel but the whole world.

Paul lived by this hope and, as a Pharisee, struggled passionately to create conditions that might contribute to the advent of this new age. His conversion came about when he experienced what he saw as the direct intervention of God in his life to announce to him that this redemptive action had already taken place in the life, death, and resurrection of Jesus of Nazareth. The new age had dawned; the movement for the liberation of humankind was already underway. In fact, the final triumph of God and thus the total transformation of the world was not only imminent; it was even now breaking into and taking shape in the present. Consequently, those who believed in Christ could live in the power of the Spirit, participate in the New Creation, and manifest the "first fruits" of it.

When Paul speaks of all this, he refers repeatedly to *resurrection:* the resurrection of Jesus from the dead and the resurrection of all the dead. When he affirms and defends this belief as the very center of Christian faith, he is also affirming, according to Beker, the total transformation of the created order: "Resurrection language properly belongs to the domain of the new age to come and is an inherent part of the transformation and recreation of all reality in the apocalyptic age" (p. 152).

The resurrection of Jesus is not some sort of "translation" or "rebirth"; it is the exaltation of someone who had been crucified by the religious and political authorities of the time. And "it foreshadows the apocalyptic general resurrection of the dead and thus the transformation of our created world" (p. 153). Belief in the resurrection thus carries with it the conviction that God has triumphed over the ultimate threat to human existence; the transformation of the world is taking place and we can be a part of it.

This perspective was so revolutionary in its implications that Paul himself often had a hard time perceiving them. But he does have some amazing things to say:

- Jesus Christ represents the fullness of human life; our goal is to be transformed into the likeness of Christ (2 Cor. 4:13). Loving one's neighbor as oneself is the law of the new age and thus the guideline for daily life.

- "Neither circumcision counts for anything, nor uncircumcision, but a new creation" (Gal. 6:15). Here the sense of a new reality being created in history was so compelling that the whole structure of law and the society ordered by it, which represented the great historical achievement of the Jewish nation, were seen as "not counting for anything."

- "There is neither Jew nor Greek, there is neither slave nor free, there is neither male nor female; for you are all one in Christ Jesus" (Gal. 3:28). This called for such a radical change in perspective that even Paul had trouble following through on it, especially when he tried to define the role of women in the church as the community of the new age.

## The Emerging Vision:
## Self-Reliant and Interdependent Nations

In biblical times, slaves, the victims of foreign domination, and poor people infected with the spirit of Jesus of Nazareth dreamed of a new future. Today Third World people in a similar situation of exploitation and domination are also dreaming of a new day. For those who have eyes to see, biblical faith and the aspirations of Third World people converge in exciting ways. Biblically oriented people are thus in a privileged position when it comes to understanding these aspirations and responding to the challenge they present to the United States.

During the colonial period — and extending uninterrupted into the present — the basic structure of First World–Third World relationships has been that of *center* to *periphery*. The major Western industrial nations have constituted the center from which economic, political, and military relations have flowed outward toward the periphery. The political structure has been that of domination; in the economic realm, the development of the countries at the center has set the terms and every effort has been made by them to have available and draw upon the resources provided by the periphery. All this has been accompanied by a certain attitude, an assumption about the superiority of the Western industrial nations. They are the center of the world, from which all good things flow. They represent civilization, and what they stand for is assumed to be universally valid.

Today, with the erosion of this myth and the weakening of these structures, the dream of the people of the Third World is not primarily to occupy some day the position held by the colonizers, but to create a new world order organized in a radically different way.

According to their vision, the new center should be constituted by *local communities becoming increasingly self-reliant* as they gain control of their own resources and use them to meet the basic needs of all their members. This fundamental shift in the economic sphere should be accompanied by an equally radical transformation in power relationships: men and women at the grassroots relating to each other in such a way as to break traditional patterns of domination and discover how to empower each other as they take increasing control over their own lives and destinies. This carries with it a growing sense of confidence in themselves and their capacities, in their own culture and history, and thus in the possibility of finding their own authentic solutions to their problems.

In other words, our Western emphasis on personal self-identity and the growth of the unique individual as the road to human fulfillment is here affirmed as the most fundamental structure for human relationships and development *in society*. On this basis, increasingly self-reliant local communities relate to others around them and provide the foundation for the organization of the economic, political, and social life of a nation.

For nations shaped by this vision, *self-determination* is the one essential condition for development. It can happen only as each country owns and controls its own resources, is in charge of its own life, and is free to find its own way. Only under these conditions can it discover how best to use its natural and human resources to offer all its citizens a chance to have a decent life. In terms of international relations, Third World nations pursuing this goal will be primarily concerned about mutually beneficial economic and political exchanges with other small and/or poor countries in their region and beyond, and from this position of relative strength discovering how to develop new relations with the more powerful industrial nations.

As I have traveled in Central and South America in recent years, I have been struck by the extent and power of this vision. I have sensed not only the attraction it has for many people in both urban and rural areas but also the way it is even now affecting political developments. I have been impressed by the witness of peasants on cooperative farms in Nicaragua as they described what it meant for them to work together for national reconstruction *on their own land*. I have been amazed by the way in which the poorest of the poor in the peripheral slums of large cities in Peru and Brazil are living out local self-reliance as they share resources and work together to meet their needs for bare survival. And I have been surprised to see that this vision is playing an important role in the thought and action of a number of new political leaders in or related to popular movements.

If this indicates the direction in which Third World peoples are moving, it is important for us in the U.S.A. to have a clear picture of what it represents. For this reason, I want to present here some of the main lines of this vision as I have come to understand it with the help of a number of Asians, Latin Americans, and Western Europeans. I am especially indebted to Professor Johan Galtung for his development of this perspective in his book *The True Worlds: A Transnational Perspective.*

1. The new center, as I mentioned earlier, is constituted by local communities, large enough to be viable economic units, moving toward increasing self-reliance. This means that the natural resources of a region must be owned and controlled locally, and that these resources be used by the people working together to meet the basic needs of all those living there. Peasants on co-operative farms care for and cultivate the land; men and women in neighboring towns concentrate their efforts at commerce and small industries. Working together, the two groups discover how to subsist as they produce more and more of the things they need. Communities functioning in this way build relations of exchange with other communities nearby and thus help each other to become more self-reliant. Regional units of this type develop similar patterns of economic relationships with each other and the economic development of the nation rests on this foundation.

All of this is so radically different from what we experience in North America that it is easy for us to dismiss it as utterly impractical and to assume that it is completely contrary to our traditional values. But as more and more Third World people suffer from undernourishment and die of hunger under the present international economic system, this restructuring of economic life around local self-reliance may turn out to be quite practical. Moreover, we may soon come to realize that such an arrangement offers vast numbers of marginal people of the world an opportunity to achieve what we value: to become entrepreneurs, to take initiatives and risks in the economic realm, and to learn to take responsibility for themselves and their future.

2. Such communities can be self-reliant only if their members participate in the exercise of public power. Or, to use the language in vogue in Latin America today, only if they become *subjects*, in charge of their own lives. This implies a fundamental restructuring of human relationships at all levels, moving away from hierarchical structures of power, in which those on top have power *over* others

and deprive them of the right to be subjects, and moving toward relationships in which people affirm and *empower each other.*

Here the revolution that has begun in male-female relations can provide a model and motivation for social reconstruction. Those of us who have discovered the vitality and richness of relationship between two persons, each of whom is growing vocationally and reaching new levels of personal fulfillment, can have some idea of the promise this quality of human relationships holds for life in community. In this regard, the experience of the Christian base communities in Latin America is of vital importance. In them, women and men who have been most marginalized and oppressed discover their worth as human beings, gain confidence in their own abilities, and take initiatives to change their situation. As their new sense of self-worth grows, they also learn how to empower each other.

For any Third World country developing along these lines of economic self-reliance and mutual empowerment of people at the grassroots, *national self-determination* will be the basic condition for authentic relations with other countries. People who learn to take charge of their own lives and work together to solve their own problems, as they gradually overcome structures of economic and political domination, will be willing to pay a high price and even to give their lives to defend their nation's right to self-determination.

3. Self-reliant communities will give increasing attention to the specific economic, social, and cultural realities around them. As they do so, they will realize the uniqueness of their own situation and the need to find their own solutions to the particular set of problems facing them. They will also give more value to their own culture, history, and national idiosyncrasy and learn not only to live in a more vital relationship with this heritage but to draw on it as a resource for social reconstruction. Ways of thinking, living, and organizing society that have evolved and been tested over centuries become an invaluable resource as they are honored and transformed in response to new challenges.

To the extent that this happens, people who formerly thought of themselves as ignorant, unprepared to live in the modern world, and incapable of contributing significantly to society begin to discover the richness of their cultural heritage and the resources they have at their disposal. As they do this, they may also come up with models for economic development and political organization quite different from the ones we have developed but more effective in their situation because they are more authentic. Likewise, their ideologies, while frequently drawing on Western liberal and Marxist thought, will use such language and categories primarily as tools for articulating the direction of their own journey as a people.

When the life of a nation revolves around self-reliant communities that provide a foundation for the material well-being of all as well as the participation of people in the exercise of public power, there will be less need for the type of state power necessary to maintain the domination of one social or ethnic group or class over another. Such communities will claim and gain increasing social space, and new patterns of international relationships, in the economic and political realms, can be created.

4. People sustained by and participating in self-reliant communities can provide a new source of desperately needed social energy for national reconstruction in the Third World. Many of us in the West come close to despair when we look at the overwhelming problems facing poor countries. What we do not realize is that the people who are suffering most in these situations can be motivated to work for solutions to their problems with tremendous energy if they discover their own worth as persons, recognize their abilities, and have a chance to work together to meet their own needs and create conditions for a better life for their children.

I have no desire to present a romantic picture of the poor or their role in social reconstruction. Those who have worked hardest at the task of empowerment of the poor are all too aware of how difficult the task is and how often leaders who emerge out of this struggle may become more interested in serving themselves than their people. But that's not the whole story. The fact that recently developed popular organizations in many poor countries are often vigorously persecuted and suppressed by the ruling elite is in itself a witness to the potential available among the poor for the solution of their problems and the transformation of their societies. Anyone who has experienced the energy and seen the initiatives taken by many basic Christian communities can never again overlook this fact. The tragic reality is that this potential is so often ignored — or destroyed — by those in power, many of whom claim they want justice and democracy but are unwilling to make the reforms necessary to move toward these goals.

This vision of a new era in international relations is still in its earliest stages of development. The task of working it out and transforming vision into reality will be a long and arduous one. But we North Americans need to be clear about one thing: the old international order, product and continuation of the basic lines set in the colonial era, is finished. The alternative to it need not be international chaos and endless war, nor should we assume that any new order can only spell defeat and loss for us. Rather, we have before us a unique opportunity to participate in creating conditions for a more just and peaceful world, which can bring new life and hope to us as well as the dispossessed. The outline of such a new world can be perceived in the midst of present struggles. The question before us is whether we as a nation can catch enough of that vision to enable us to work for it rather than spend our energies fighting against those trying to bring it into being. An ongoing dialogue with the biblical witness mentioned above can, we believe, contribute significantly to this rebirth of vision.

## Chapter 6

# A NEW FUTURE FOR THREE WORLDS

THE BIBLICAL ORIENTATION toward a future of promise may speak directly to the aspirations of Third World people. But does it have anything to say to us? They envision and struggle for a *new world order* that would open up new possibilities for them, economically and politically. But their dream of a future of national self-determination could well mean, for us, a loss of much that we dreamed of in the past and were able to achieve. If this is the prospect ahead of us, how can we focus our attention on a new world order or become involved in a struggle for it?

In relation to this question, the Bible also has something to say. It suggests that those who benefit from a given status quo can indeed dream of a better future because the struggle of those at the bottom holds the promise of bringing into being a more just and more human world for all. Slaves living in Egypt are called by Yahweh to move out and create a new society in a promised land. In their struggle to overcome the oppression they know, they can become a "light to the nations," a "city set on a hill." The Reign of God, as portrayed by Jesus, belongs to the poor. But they are destined to be the salt of the earth and the light of the world as they strive for a new day of justice and peace for all. According to St. Paul, in Jesus Christ a process of reconciliation, aiming at the redemption of nature and society, has begun and is moving forward. In each of these instances, the issue is not whether the envisioned future will bring new life to those who benefit from the status quo, but only whether they will be able to perceive that what is offered to them is life.

73

For Jesus, those who are rich can enter God's Reign if they "go through the eye of a needle," if they are willing to "sell all that they have and give to the poor" as they follow the One who is crucified by the wealthy and powerful. Paul expresses all this most dramatically when he declares that those who want to live in the new age must die to their past in order to experience resurrection, i.e., a richness of life so different from everything they have known previously that it could not have been imagined or expected by those living within the bounds of the past.

This way of understanding things is so contrary to our usual way of thinking that we can easily dismiss it as completely impractical, if not absurd. Except for one fact: *some people in this country have put this to the test in recent years and are giving a compelling witness to its truth.* In their openness to the biblical witness and through their participation in a community of faith, they come to see that the status quo from which they benefit is more death-producing than life-giving. As they look honestly and critically at the world around them, they begin to yearn for a better future. As they learn to let loose of what they have and who they have been, they are surprised by possibilities they did not know existed before. And to the extent that they experience this change in their personal lives and in society, they find themselves thinking about international relations in the same way. Out of this process a passion for fundamental change in our foreign policy is being born and nourished.

I have seen this happening with some well-to-do church people who have spent a few weeks in close contact with the poor in India or Haiti, gone to Central America for short visits, or become involved in programs to help the homeless or other marginal groups in the U.S.A. I have also seen this happen with many of us who have spent years living and working in Third World countries as we have tried to understand and respond to the dynamics of a rapidly changing world.

I began my missionary career living in a large house in a wealthy neighborhood and going to work in a chauffeur-driven car; during our last assignment in Central America, my wife and I lived in one room with a poor family. During my early years as a missionary, I had a clearly defined position of authority in an educational institution owned and directed by a North American mission agency. When I now go to Latin America, I go at the invitation of groups or institutions there, to work under their direction, knowing that I am there primarily to learn rather than to teach.

What to me is most significant in all this is the fact that I find the present arrangement much more interesting and rewarding. I now know that North American-dominated institutions not only denied Latins the chance to think, act, and create something for themselves; they also put us as North Americans in positions in which we could not function effectively. As people in diverse situations got in touch with their own potential and found their own way, I found a place for myself working as a partner in projects I would never have been able to imagine or carry forward. As I made a greater effort to enter into and learn from another culture, my life was enriched; their utopian vision contributed to the rebirth of vision on my part.

Such individual experiences may suggest new options open to us as a nation in our relation with Third World countries. As they sharpen their vision of a future of national self-determination and interdependence, they offer us a chance to discover how to live for the future as a nation in the world of nations. Confronted by their vision, we can perceive more clearly the destructiveness of present relations of domination *for us.* We can explore ways of sharing our knowledge and experience with national leaders who understand their situation much better than we can ever hope to do. Little by little we will become aware of the benefits we receive from such relations of mutuality. Eventually we may find ourselves affirming a future world of self-determining and interdependent nations as *our* future as well.

I want to suggest here six areas in which a change in our policy in support of the vision of Third World peoples could offer us a new future:

## The Possibilities of Power

*With our tremendous economic resources — our wealth, our economic power, our technological know-how — we can take the initiative in honoring the right of these nations to own and control their natural resources, their agricultural and industrial production and distribution, and to use them to meet the needs and serve the interests of their people.*

I realize that present economic relationships are moving in the opposite direction, undermining rather than laying a foundation for national self-reliance. The colonial pattern of foreign ownership and control — of mines, railroads, banana plantations, etc. — has given way to massive penetration of large multinational corporations, agribusiness ownership of large tracts of land, with production primarily for export, and subcontracting by multinationals in order to take advantage of the cheap labor available in poor countries.

No matter how powerful this trend may be at present, we must raise serious questions about what will happen in the future if it continues. Nations with limited resources and expanding populations will find themselves less and less able to develop their economies to meet the most basic needs of their people. Unrestricted expansion of multinational corporations tends to integrate the economy of poor countries into that of the Western industrial world, oriented toward very different goals. Production for export by agribusiness works against the building up of local farming communities making the best possible use of the land in order to produce food for themselves and their neighbors. Subcontracting, while providing jobs for women and men who might otherwise be unemployed, is oriented toward production for the artificially stimulated international consumer market, not toward resourcing local communities interested in doing everything possible to help themselves.

We now know that this process has brought us to a point where one billion people are living in poverty. We cannot escape the possibility that, continuing along this line, millions will die of starvation each year. Many of those most deprived will turn, in desperation, to violence and terror. And we will find ourselves spending an even higher percentage of our national budget on weapons of war but with no hope of living in peace.

Our biblical faith doesn't provide us with a model for a new international economic order. But by focussing our attention on future possibility, it allows us to see the absurdity of the present arrangement as well as the moral and intellectual bankruptcy of a society locked into such destructive patterns yet incapable of imagining an alternative to them. It frees us to be open to and search for other options and to encourage groups, in the university and the church, in government and business, to go about that task. This is an important contribution now being made by Christians working with study and research centers in various parts of Central and South America. More contact with them could encourage us to be more involved in similar efforts here at home as well.

## New Leaders for New Societies

*We can learn how to relate to a new generation of leaders of self-reliant nations and, as we do so, find that they have something to contribute to us.*

National self-determination, built on the foundation of communities and regions moving toward economic and political self-reliance, brings with it a new type of leader with whom our representatives will be engaged around the conference table. If we look closely at the social forces now involved in efforts at economic development and social reconstruction along these lines, we can get a clear idea of who these people are and will be. Some are the sons and daughters of the dominant elites who, in the face of the suffering of the people around them, have decided to change sides. Others are women and men from the middle and lower classes who have had a chance to get a university education and enter the professions but are committed to supporting the struggle of their people. As popular movements among the rural and urban poor come to play an important role in economic and social development, leaders emerging from these movements will come to the fore not only within the nation but in its international dealings as well.

This new leadership will be quite different from the elite with whom we have traditionally related. Most of them will not be graduates of our Ivy League schools nor those whom our diplomats and politicians have known in corporate or academic circles, but that fact does not make them anti-American. They will be committed to creating a new economic and social order serving the interests of the poor majority, but this does not mean that most of them are bound by a rigid leftist ideology. They will not tolerate Western domination of their countries, nor relations that smack of paternalism, yet they know that it is in their national interest to cultivate positive relationships with the U.S.A. For a time, their resentment of past injustices and their passion for bringing about radical change may make constructive interaction difficult; in the long run, a willingness on our part to develop patterns of mutual respect and interdependence will make it possible to build relations of mutual trust and even of solidarity in a common struggle. At present, the major burden is on us: to demonstrate that we as a nation support their attempts to build a society moving toward greater social justice and democracy, and that we can relate to them as equals and as partners.

## Partners in Struggle

*Self-reliant people, in control of their own destiny as a nation, will struggle energetically to find THEIR OWN SOLUTIONS TO THEIR PARTICULAR PROBLEMS. As we share their vision and honor their struggle, we will find a new role for ourselves as their partners in efforts to overcome poverty and develop patterns of economic and social organization that we ourselves could not imagine or hope to establish.*

When national development is oriented toward the maximum participation of the people themselves in meeting their needs, making use of the materials and resources available to them, only those who know and live in a particular situation, who are part of that culture and history, can figure out how this type of development can take place. Only they can come up with patterns of economic and social organization that will make the best use of local resources as well as appropriate technology. Only as a people becoming subjects are struggling to find their own way can they take *ownership* of their project of national reconstruction, and thus be willing to devote their energies to the project and to sacrifice for it.

Moreover, when the central focus is on self-reliant communities that can provide the basis for regions and nations becoming increasingly self-sufficient, this calls for a type of economic development and social organization about which we know very little. Our society is still headed in a different direction as small farmers lose their land and people in local communities have less and less control over what happens there. The poorest people in the slums of São Paulo or Lima, and those who work most closely with them, may have richer insight into how they can work together to survive economically and how best to organize their community life than experts from North America.

Those who are working out Paulo Freire's theories about adult education may know much more about education for empowerment of the dispossessed than those trained in our schools of education. Those who believe that they can imagine and create new and more human forms of social organization are more likely to have the vision and energy necessary for this task than those who are content to reproduce solutions worked out elsewhere.

Although we may not be aware of it, scores of groups and centers are now working on these issues throughout the Third World. As I have traveled in Central and South America in recent years, I have been amazed not just by the number of such groups I have found but by the quality of work many of them are doing. Brilliant men and women with excellent training in various disciplines — many of them with graduate degrees from universities in North America or Western Europe — are working on economic, social, and political problems and are producing new models and projects for development. Very often they are directly related to popular movements, learning from them as they make their knowledge available to them. They frequently maintain close contacts and collaborate with similar groups in other countries, not only in their region but in Europe and the United States, as well as with progressive churches and religious movements locally and internationally. The resources they provide are available to governmental and private agencies who want to make use of them. If they are not used more, it is because those now in power lack the interest and the will to seek and implement creative solutions to the problems they and their countries are facing.

Out of all this may come patterns of economic, social, and political organization quite different from our own. This is inevitable if the movement toward democracy in Third World countries means using the resources of each to serve the interests of the majority and giving the people at the bottom increasing opportunities to participate in society.

Our economic system has aroused the aspirations of people for a better life but has not made it possible for the poor majority in most Third World countries. And while we have given great emphasis to democracy, we have continued to support the small and powerful elites who deny the majority an opportunity to participate in public life. Where Marxist regimes have come into power, they have done a great deal to overcome poverty and provide basic services for all, but have thus far failed to restructure power relations so as to give the people at the bottom increasing opportunities to shape their future.

Given this situation, the emergence and consolidation of new popular movements and the proposals for new solutions coming from those identified with them offer a great deal of promise for the future. The new social and economic structures emerging from their efforts may not be what we would like to see, but if they represent authentic responses to local situations and move toward the goals of economic well-being for the people and participatory democracy, they will help lay the foundation for a new era of peace among nations. Self-confident, self-reliant people capable of finding their own way are more likely to create conditions for social stability, live in peace with their neighbors, and resist all attempts of foreign powers to dominate or manipulate them.

### A New Vision for the U.S.A.

*Our contact with the Third World can help us to envision a new future for our own country, that of interdependent, self-reliant communities creating a more self-sufficient nation, thus reducing our dependence on outside resources.*

As Third World people succeed in their struggle to gain more control over their lives in a world dominated by enormous impersonal economic and political institutions, our contact with them can help us to look more closely at what these same forces are doing to us. Uncontrolled large-scale industrial and technological development, the growth of conglomerates with the concentration of power that goes with it, the centralized bureaucracies of corporations and government: these developments leave us with a sense of powerlessness and deprive us of real control over our lives and our communities. Within these structures, relationships between employer and employee, producer and consumer, those who provide services and those who receive them, tend to be bureaucratic in nature. Work has little meaning; those who provide services need take little responsibility for what they do. Caught within a system that no longer works to our advantage, confronting forces over which we have little control, we find ourselves isolated, frustrated, and insecure.

In this situation, contact with the Third World and with the utopian vision of our religious heritage could lead us to believe in the possibility of creating a more human society here at home. Local communities can achieve a degree of self-reliance as they make use of appropriate technology, decentralize the production of energy, and discover how teams of women and men can work together to create small-scale cooperative or profit-sharing enterprises through which to meet many of their basic needs. We can work together to provide services for each other and learn how to be less dependent on large-scale service programs. We can develop patterns of grassroots, town-hall democracy that will enable people in local communities to work together to provide educational and community services, have clean air and water, care for the underprivileged and abandoned, the sick and the elderly. We can use our knowledge, our technological know-how, and our energies to create a society in which self-reliance is a way of life and people develop relationships of mutual responsibility.

This vision of a new future for North America is very much alive among small groups in many places, groups hard at work making it a reality through cooperative efforts in small-scale agriculture, manufacturing, and the provision of services. Their efforts include political action to challenge the trend toward greater centralization and to pass legislation favoring small businesses and local production cooperatives, and seeking to make government funds available to local groups committed to caring for themselves. One interesting development along this line is a special fund established a few years ago by the Canadian government to help local organizations of elderly people take initiatives in providing services for other elderly persons in need.

To the extent that this dream shapes our society, we will be prepared to live more creatively in an interdependent world. We will learn how to become economically more self-sufficient as a nation and to depend less on resources from outside. When we live more securely in stable, self-reliant communities, we will have a new freedom to face the changes called for in our relations with other countries. As we become excited about creating a new quality of life in community for ourselves, we will be able to relate positively to the struggles of Third World nations; more than that, we will find ourselves making a major contribution to world peace as we draw on our historical experience, our knowledge, and our resources for the construction of a new world order.

### Responding to Marxism

*To the extent that we are attuned to the utopian vision of Third World peoples and are ourselves captivated by a similar vision of a new world order, we will be prepared as a nation to face and respond to the challenge of Marxism as well as the dangers of Soviet penetration in the Third World.*

At the present time, our lack of such a vision constitutes our major handicap in dealing with the Third World, and all our military might cannot make up for this lack. Without it, we fail to see that national self-determination is their most cherished aspiration and are incapable of relating to national leaders and political movements committed to transforming their societies in line with this vision. Without it we are crippled in our engagement with Marxism because we fail to realize that a vision of a transformed society is at the heart of that ideology and movement and is a major source of its appeal.

Lacking this vision, our policy cannot go beyond the defense of the international status quo; our pursuit of it makes us appear before the poor people of the world as the enemy of all they hope for. In our opposition to Marxism, we may mouth lofty ideals of freedom and democracy, but what comes through is our fear of change in the direction of social justice.

Having lost the orientation toward the future that inspired our nation in the beginning, we deny to other countries the very thing our founders dreamed of two centuries ago. We also violate the norms of international relations we have helped to establish over the years. In our attempts to overthrow the government of Nicaragua, we have refused to accept the jurisdiction of the World Court, and thus undermined its authority; we have also gone against the charter of the Organization of American States, which declares that no nation has the right to intervene in the internal affairs of another.

Our continued opposition to movements and governments attempting to develop economic structures serving the interests of the poor majority because they are or might become Marxist only serves to augment the appeal of Marxism among those who can no longer tolerate injustice and oppression. Every time we intervene in another country in violation of their struggle for national self-determination — on the grounds that they are or will be used by the Soviet Union — we create more favorable conditions for the extension of Soviet influence.

If, on the other hand, we are engaged in transforming our own society in line with a compelling vision of a new world order, we will be able to relate to Third World nations with a new sense of confidence and face the challenge of international Communism without being afraid of those who struggle for justice. We will honor the struggle for national self-determination and support those who are involved in it, recognizing that they aspire to much of what we fought our war of independence to achieve. We will also be able to see that their struggle today is somewhat different from our struggle then. If their goals are similar to those of the American Revolution, they are also forced to struggle against U.S. economic and political domination. The fact that, in many countries, the vast majority of people are impoverished and exploited by a small oligarchy means that their revolutions will bring about fundamental changes in the economic order we have supported until now. And the emergence of popular movements among the dispossessed opens the way for greater grassroots participation in the political process than we now have and for the creation of new political institutions.

As our obsession with the preservation of the status quo gives way to excitement about a new world order, we will find ourselves standing with and supporting leaders committed to national reconstruction. As we engage in dialogue with them, we may find that many of them do not fit our stereotype of a Marxist. We will perceive that our major concern should not be whether they are ideological Marxists of one type or another, but whether they are faithful to a utopian vision of economic well-being for all and the participation of the people at the bottom in the exercise of public power. Rather than pushing them toward reliance on Soviet support to survive, we will encourage them to take their vision of international nonalignment seriously and work it out in relation to both superpowers.

Whatever may happen in the relations between the U.S.A. and Nicaragua in the near future, the policy we have pursued will become a symbol for many people around the world of our failure to take advantage of an opportunity offered us to explore new directions in our policy toward the Third World.

During the months I spent in Nicaragua in 1984, I was convinced that many leaders of the revolution, as well as their grass-roots supporters, were committed to developing an economic and political order that would be quite different not only from what countries in that region had known before, but also from the Cuban model. I was impressed by the type of mixed economy being developed, by the farm cooperatives and the control the peasants had over them, and especially by the participation of the people in a variety of popular movements and the fact that national leaders seemed to encourage it. Sympathetic North American support could have contributed to a fuller development of such an alternative and strengthened the hands of those committed to it.

I also found a strong desire, on the part of many of the leaders I got to know, to follow a policy of international nonalignment, with "diversified dependency" rather than depending on one major power or a small number of ideologically similar countries. A willingness on our part to encourage and support such nonalignment would have given us an opportunity to find out whether or not this possibility existed and how far a government of national reconstruction might go in carrying it out.

What our government has done and is now doing can only undermine these efforts and strengthen the hand of those who are more doctrinaire. Our vicious denunciations of the Sandinistas, with such gross distortion of the picture of what is happening there, and our support of the brutal defenders of a repudiated order, who have no basis of support in their country and no viable project for its future: all these things serve only to discredit us and any ideals we say we stand for. In the long run, we are creating favorable conditions for the very things we most fear: doctrinaire Marxism and greater Soviet penetration in the area.

Sooner or later, we must come to realize that the emerging utopian vision represents the major reason why Third World struggles cannot be understood within the framework of the East-West struggle. In fact, it could well become the major force carrying all of us beyond the narrow confines of that struggle. For this vision of Third World people, together with their efforts to create a new society, represents a fundamental challenge to both the Soviet Union and the United States, to traditional Marxist and capitalist ideologies. Stable and peaceful Third World countries moving toward social justice and participatory democracy could contribute decisively to a new era in international relations in which the struggle between the U.S.A. and the Soviet Union would become less dangerous and assume less importance, and the two superpowers would be challenged to dedicate their energies and their wealth to more constructive ends.

## Beyond the Nation-State

*Those who catch the vision of a future world order will question our traditional assumptions about the importance and role of the nation-state and seek ways by which U.S. policy can go beyond the limitations imposed on it by that ideology.*

By now, we are well aware of the fact that we live in a global village. All the peoples of the world are living in close contact with each other, interrelated and interdependent. Multinational corporations and communication systems transcend national limits. Polluted air and nuclear fall-out ignore national boundaries. Every military conflict has the potential of producing a world conflagration.

Sooner or later, we will be forced to recognize that, in such a world, we can make progress toward the solution of our major problems only as we develop supranational authorities to deal with them. The possibility of a more human existence on this planet, to say nothing of human survival, depends upon the cooperative efforts of people of goodwill around the world to create such international institutions capable of moving beyond the narrow limits of national self-interest.

Parallel with this, the vision of self-reliant communities in which women and men empower each other to take increasing control of their lives is leading many diverse groups to seek relative autonomy and build relations of collaboration with each other. In such a world, tribal, ethnic, and racial groups will demand increasing space in which to develop their own economic and political structures. Other communities will come together around a common commitment to a particular way of life or type of society. National units will continue to function for a long time, but their role will be reduced as more natural and authentic groups of people and communities emerge.

From this perspective of a possible more human world order, the ideology of the nation-state, which gives absolute value to the pursuit of national self-interest through the enhancement of power, no longer makes sense. With the struggle of Third World people for national independence, the powerful nations of the world, in the pursuit of their national interest, deny the little people of the world the right to pursue the same goal. Rather than serving the self-interest of the people of our own and other Western nations, it functions to sustain and increase the power of the few, at the same time that it supports a structure of international relations that is incapable of solving our most urgent international problems. As Robert Johansen puts it, in *The National Interest and the Human Interest,*

> In a system devoid of central guidance, when states compete with one another to achieve national economic and political advantages, officials will not disarm, wealth will not be used rationally to maximize fulfillment of human needs, the drive for overseas political influence and economic exploitation will ride roughshod over respect for human rights, and nationally selfish exploitation of resources plus environmentally hazardous (though economically cheap) waste disposal will occur. A competitive situation encourages those governments with the most economic and political resources to protect and increase their advantages without much regard for the plight of those with fewer resources. (p. 390)

Sooner or later, a system that is so incapable of solving our most urgent problems and fails to serve the interests of so many people in the world must be repudiated on moral grounds. For Professor Johansen, "Current expressions of great power nationalism and the self-seeking policies of sovereign states will be eventually understood to be as morally outrageous as racism is viewed today" (p. 392). If none of us can choose either the race or the nation into which we are born, "privileges that automatically accrue to one's nationality (or race) because of economic and political structures cannot be justified either by reason or by the most widely professed moral philosophies of the world" (pp. 392–393).

All this has a special significance for us as North Americans. When we pursue national self-interest by unrestrained use of our power in relation to poor and weak nations, we violate one of the most fundamental principles on which our nation was built: the conviction that the abuse of power can be checked only as those who are the victims of it are empowered and find ways to exercise countervailing power. When we abandon our own ideals and deny other nations the very thing we most cherish, we set the stage for those international forces we most fear to appear as defenders of what we have historically stood for.

By giving absolute value to the sovereign state and pursuing policies serving the narrow interest of our nation in its dominant position within the present system, our policy-makers are unable to respond to pressures for change coming from the Third World. Rather than taking steps toward a new international order in which tensions might be reduced, they insist on doing everything possible to preserve the status quo. When they meet with increasing opposition, they interpret this to mean that we are living in a cruel and dangerous Hobbesian world in which people are constantly at war with each other. Victims of such an ideology, they espouse a deep pessimism about the future of the world at the same time that they justify using all their energies to make the present system function as long as possible.

On the other hand, those capable of envisioning a future world that can come into being only after the collapse of the present system of sovereign nation-states, can take steps now to lay the foundation for it. The erosion of this system can open the way for people to live in more secure and peaceful communities as they move toward greater self-sufficiency and develop patterns of interdependence with others. At the same time, those guided by the vision of a new world order can take steps toward the development of supranational authorities to deal with a variety of global problems.

As some of the underlying causes of violent conflict between communities and nations are dealt with, the world of the future may not turn out to be as cruel or as dangerous as many of those now in power predict it will be, even in the midst of overwhelming economic and social problems. Third World nations may discover that they don't have to buy the ideology of Western or Communist nationalism or adopt a model of nation-building that is already obsolete. They can use their energies to imagine and develop new structures of economic and political life, and new patterns of relationships among nations. They can thus set an example for the First and Second Worlds as they point the way to the future.

Chapter 7

# THE BIBLICAL SOURCES
# OF REVOLUTIONARY FERMENT

SOONER OR LATER, we North Americans may pay more attention to the plight of the poor masses of the world and realize that it is in our national interest to support their struggle for life. In our interaction with them, we may catch the contagion of their dreams for the future and find ourselves dreaming of a new world order. We have a more serious problem, however, when those working for these goals insist that they can hope to achieve them only through *social revolution.*

This is, of course, a natural reaction on our part, given our present situation. Most of us live in relative comfort and economic security and are recognized as persons of worth — within the established order. We are thus concerned about preserving a system providing us with such benefits rather than overthrowing it. We have been brought up in a society that not only offers the majority of its citizens a reasonable level of economic well-being but guarantees basic human rights, undergirded by a social contract. We have taken pride in the fact that we live in an open society, which we believe is moving toward a better future as we struggle to transform it and find the means by which that can be done. We may, from time to time, be disturbed by the gap we perceive between the reality we live and the ideals we profess, but that rarely leads us to challenge these basic assumptions.

As we pointed out earlier, the situation in Third World countries is often quite different. The established order serves the interests of an extremely small minority while the great majority live in desperate subhuman conditions. Political power is in the hands of a small oligarchy, often in alliance with, if not directly dependent upon, the military who serve their interests. When the deprived majority bring pressures for change in the political structures or for social reforms, they are repressed, often brutally. Under these conditions, the masses of poor people become poorer; all roads to the transformation of society are blocked; and those who find the status quo intolerable see no possibility for change short of the revolutionary overthrow of the established order.

Faced by this situation we would do well to remember that when the colonists in what is now the United States of America were struggling for national self-determination, they stood out as the world's leading revolutionary people. Those who drafted our Declaration of Independence were convinced that the established structure of relations with Great Britain was so destructive of their most cherished rights as human beings that it had to be overthrown. They declared that men and women are endowed with such inalienable rights as life, liberty, and the pursuit of happiness; and that "whenever any form of government becomes destructive of these ends, it is the right of the people to alter and abolish it and to institute a new government."

Our Founders saw this revolution as representing a radical break with the past, opening up the possibility of creating a new human being living in a society such as had not been created until that time, a *novus ordo saeclorum*. For Thomas Paine, it meant a chance to "begin the world over again," a situation which "hath not happened since the days of Noah until now." They also saw this new social order as having a worldwide subversive influence, and rejoiced in it. Alexander Hill Everett, a major American historian in the early nineteenth century, spoke of all those struggling to bring a new world into existence as "our brothers," and saw the influence of our example and achievements shaking up the whole world: "Behold the mighty spirit of Reform striding like a giant through the civilized world and trampling down established abuses at every step" (quoted by Kohn 1957, 35).

Moreover, we tend to forget the fact that our nation fought not just one but two revolutionary wars. The Civil War has been referred to as the "Second American Revolution" (Charles Beard) or the "Last Capitalist Revolution" (Barrington Moore), because of what it did to break the hold of the plantation system and create favorable conditions for the rapid development of industry as well as democratic institutions.

In fact, our Western democracies may owe much more than we imagine to the English and French Revolutions and the American Civil War. This is the claim made some years ago by Barrington Moore in his book, *The Social Origins of Dictatorship and Democracy.* In it, he shows how the radical break caused by these revolutions not only created conditions for capitalism to flourish but also made democracy possible. In Germany and Japan, where such revolutions from below did not occur, the commercial and industrial class relied on dissident elements of the older and still dominant ruling classes to put through the changes needed for modern industrial society, but this led to fascism. On the other hand, in England the Parliament as well as stable economic institutions for the development of industry are the product of a "violent past." "The violent destruction of the *ancien régime* was a crucial step for France on the long road toward democracy" (p. 108). And as for the U.S.A., Moore concludes that if the Southern plantation system had continued, and been able to establish itself in the West by the middle of the nineteenth century, "the US would have been in the position of some modernizing countries today, with a latifundia economy, a dominant antidemocratic aristocracy, unable and unwilling to push forward toward political democracy" (p. 153).

A new appreciation of our revolutionary history could help us relate to the social upheavals taking place around us. But if there is anything in our heritage that compels us to look favorably on revolution, it comes primarily from the Bible rather than the Declaration of Independence. To be sure, the Bible does not use our modern language about revolution. But from the Book of Exodus to the Apocalypse of John, we have the story of a people whose God calls them, time and again, to break out of bondage to the past and leads them in the construction of a radically new social order. In earlier chapters, we focussed primarily on the Exodus story, the teachings of the prophets, and the gospel narratives of the life of Jesus of Nazareth and have seen how central, in each of them, is a burning concern for the poor as well as an intense longing for a future world of justice and peace. But we should not overlook the fact that these three major sections of the Scriptures also point clearly in the direction of the radical transformation of society, or revolution.

## The Exodus: "A Program for Revolution"

In the opening paragraph of *Exodus and Revolution,* Michael Walzer calls attention to the fact that "revolution has often been imagined as an enactment of the Exodus and the Exodus has often been imagined as a program for revolution" (p. ix). Later on, he goes further to claim that the Exodus story has provided the impetus for every social revolution in modern times. The reason for this is not hard to find. In a world in which the gods were the major bulwark of the established order, Yahweh, the God of the Israelites, not only leads a slave rebellion but covenants with them to build a radically new society that should serve as a model of justice for the world. This story thus not only highlights the central elements making up a revolutionary struggle; by relating them to a God conceived as Creator and Lord of all nations and peoples, it suggests that social revolutions play a central role in historical development, in a world in which such a God is actively present. The Exodus, as a program for revolution, focuses attention on three major elements in this type of struggle:

1. The God who hears the cry of sorely oppressed slaves leads them in a rebellion against the established order of the pharaoh. The Israelites can bring about a redistribution of goods and create the order of justice Yahweh calls for only after a decisive *break* with the established order. They must not only become disloyal to the pharaoh; they have to *get out of Egypt.* Slaves must be set free; only then can they have a human life. The structures of kingly power and tyrannical rule must be broken; thus the rejoicing in the destruction of chariots and horses, symbols of that oppressive domination. The God of the people of Israel is present in a cloud and a pillar of fire, leading them away from what they had into a new and unexplored land.

For the pharaoh, Moses and his associates are subversive characters, dangerous revolutionaries, who today might be denounced as terrorists. But God takes the side of the slaves, who see what is happening as a divine miracle bringing liberation from bondage. They join with Deborah in singing subversive songs, rejoicing that their oppressors have been defeated (Exod. 15).

2. The God who leads a slave people out of Egypt calls them to engage in a long and arduous effort at national reconstruction aiming at the creation of an economic, social, and political order

radically different from anything known at that time. In order to have the freedom to do this, they must not only leave Egypt; they must also overcome those who rule in the land to which they are going. And God insists that they struggle to free themselves from the remnants of Egypt they still carry within themselves: their hankering after "the fleshpots of Egypt" as well as the temptation to turn to Egyptian gods when the burden of creating a new world seems too great to bear.

Moses, as the founder of a new society, carries on a tremendous struggle with the people for forty years to establish a way of life that, in its radicality, can hardly be matched even by modern socialist revolutions. At the center is Yahweh's command to love one's neighbor as oneself (Lev. 19:18). When spelled out, this means a radical redistribution of land and goods, moving in the direction of an egalitarian society. By following God's commandments, all will be able to eat bread without scarcity. lacking nothing (Deut. 8:9). They will live in a society without oppression: no longer will one build and another inhabit, one plant and another eat (Isa. 65:22). Israel will also become a nation in which all the people will have a position of worth and be participants. For God starts a new order with the consent of newly freed people; God makes a covenant with *all the people:* "all the men of Israel, your little ones, your wives, and the sojourner who is in your camp, both he who hews your wood and he who draws your water" (Deut. 29:11l). In fact, it is Yahweh's desire that all be raised up to the position of prominence occupied by priests and prophets. What we have here is not a utopian dream of an unachievable ideal world but a tremendous historical effort to construct a just society, attentive to the needs and yearnings of all people, in obedience to a divine command.

3. The struggle of the people to create this type of society produces a historical dynamic moving toward greater prosperity and security as well as favorable relations with other nations: in other words, it produces *a movement toward life.* The betrayal of these goals will set in motion a process leading to economic disaster, social conflict, and national humiliation at the hands of enemies: it produces *a movement toward death.* In his last public appearance before his people, Moses declares: "I have set before you this day life and good, death and evil. If you obey the commandments of the Lord your God . . . then you shall live and multiply; but if your

hearts turn away, and you will not hear, . . . you shall perish" (Deut. 30:15–18).

Spiritual discernment is a matter of perceiving whether a society, at a given time and place, is moving in the direction of life or death. For the movement toward death means nothing less than a return to the intolerable conditions of oppression in Egypt. As Moses put it dramatically: "The Lord will bring you back in ships to Egypt, a journey which I promised that you should never make again; and there you shall offer yourselves for sale to your enemies as male and female slaves, but no man will buy you" (Deut. 30:68). On the other hand, the faithful Israelites in each new generation will participate in the movement toward life as they once again break out of the bondage represented by Egypt and engage in the struggle for national transformation. "In every generation a man is obliged to consider himself as if he had moved out of Egypt" (Mishna Pesachim, X, 5).

## The Witness of the Prophets: God Tears Down and Rebuilds

Some centuries later, the people of Israel faced a series of severe national crises, which they found it difficult if not impossible to understand. Their nation had its origin in a great historical event, the Exodus from Egypt; they considered themselves to be God's chosen people and were convinced that their God would thus protect them from their enemies and guarantee their future as a nation. And yet, their very existence was threatened by internal crises as well as repeated attacks by the armies of neighboring empires.

From the midst of this situation, a succession of extraordinary individuals emerged with a shocking and profoundly subversive message. The Hebrew prophets declared that the God who liberated a slave people from pharaoh has one supreme goal for history, the establishment of a world of justice, in which all people, beginning with those at the bottom, will have the possibility of a fully human life. Israel, called to fulfill this mission in the world, has failed at it. Therefore, God is judging this people and will have to destroy a disobedient nation in order to move history toward this goal.

Jeremiah put it most dramatically in his description of his call to be a prophet: "The Lord said to me: . . . I have set you this day over nations and over kingdoms, to pluck up and to break down, to destroy and to overthrow, to build and to plant" (1:10). Gerhard von Rad, in his masterful study of the theology of the prophets, concludes that the central element in their perspective was a sense of imminent judgment on the present order and the expectation that, beyond it, Yahweh would bring about a new era for his people. In other words, the prophets introduce *radical discontinuity* as an important positive factor in historical development; in certain circumstances, there is no other way to create a more just society.

These men were not only overwhelmed by the centrality and depth of God's concern for justice; they were also totally convinced that this God will let nothing block its achievement in history. This gave them an extraordinary freedom in dealing with the past. If the new Word of judgment they proclaimed contradicted what they had said earlier, that was because their God was acting in the same way. Yahweh was not only speaking a new and different Word to them; this God was willing, in the words of von Rad, to "revoke his historical design," to tear down God's own work in history.

As the prophets struggled to understand and live out the implications of all this, they came to conclusions that, to this day, are shocking. In responding to the call to be prophets, they were compelled to make a dramatic break with their own past. "So deep is the gulf that separates the prophets from their past that none of their previous social relationships are carried over into the new way of life" (von Rad 1965, 58). God's message to the people is that they should not focus their attention even on what God has done in the past but rather look toward what can and will happen in the future: "Remember not the former things nor consider the things of old. Behold I am doing a new thing; now it springs forth, do you not perceive it?" (Isa. 43:18–19). Consequently, the existing religious institutions were denounced as invalid and the religious practices of the people stood under judgment.

If this was the case with religious structures, then no social or political order could claim to be sacred. God's judgment on Israel meant the end of the established social order. The prophets declare that suddenly, in an instant, ruin will overtake a whole generation: God will destroy God's own people, leaving only a pitiful remnant. The break will be so sharp that the new state beyond it cannot be seen as a continuation of what went before.

All this destruction is not, however, the last word. It is rather the prelude to a new era; it opens the way for the creation of a new order of justice. God is indeed doing a new thing. The only hope for the people of Israel lies in a new action in history; only thus can they fulfill their historical mission. The prophets find meaning in contemporary events not so much by analogies with what happened in the past as by looking forward to events planned in the sovereign freedom of God. As von Rad puts it, their whole preaching is characterized by an unrivalled ability to respond to new historical developments and to point toward the eventual appearance of the qualitatively new: a new entry into the land, the appearance of a new David, a new Zion, a new covenant.

For the prophets, all the nations of the world, not just Israel, have both the vocation and the opportunity to move through history on the road from bondage to liberation, from oppression to justice for all, beginning with those at the bottom. But in order to follow that road, from time to time they may have to break with their past and make a new beginning, overthrow an established order and take on the task of creating a new society. Or, as the prophets predicted for Israel, they would have to be scattered and gathered again.

### Jesus: The Messiah Who Is "Making All Things New"

Jesus belongs to the people of the Exodus, whose God freed them from slavery in Egypt; a nation denounced by the prophets — and later destroyed — for having departed from that vocation; a people who have lived for six hundred years under foreign domination and are desperately yearning for a new Exodus from bondage.

Jesus situates himself fully within that history and speaks directly to the suffering and yearning of his people. He refuses to organize and lead a political movement to overthrow the Roman rulers, but does something that has had, across the centuries, a much more revolutionary impact: by his life and his words, together with the interpretation given to them by the gospel writers, Jesus calls into question the very foundations of the established order — whether it be religious or political — and focuses attention on a new order of justice already breaking into the present. Thus, Jesus inspires those who would follow him to adopt a revolutionary approach to every established order of oppression and he awakens in them a passion for justice and for a quality of human life that can serve as a disturbing ferment within revolutionary societies as well.

Here I want to call attention to several elements in his life and thought which led his disciples to take this stance:

1. In their new state of bondage, the people of the Exodus came to believe that their God would once again intervene in their history to set them free. They yearned for the coming of a *Messiah* who would bring in a new era of justice, in which they would once again enjoy the peace that comes with the elimination of oppression. This longing had reached a high pitch at the time when Jesus lived. He took up this theme and gave it a central place in his teaching; he drew repeatedly on the messianic imagery to interpret who he was and what he was doing. He allowed his disciples to speak of him as the Messiah, and the Christian movement affirmed this by calling him the Christ.

What this meant is clearly stated in the Magnificat, found in the first chapter of the Gospel of Luke, which one Catholic scholar calls the *leitmotif* of that Gospel. In it, Mary declares that, with the coming of the Messiah, God "has scattered the proud in the imagination of their hearts, he has put down the mighty from their thrones, and exalted those of low degree; he has filled the hungry with good things, and the rich he has sent empty away" (1:51–53). The transformation wrought by the Messiah is indeed as radical in its implications as the first Exodus. It means nothing less than the overthrow of those structures favoring the proud, the powerful and the wealthy and the creation of a new society raising up and serving the interests of those at the bottom. But with Jesus of Nazareth, the subversive impact of the Messiah goes far beyond the Egyptian pharaoh or the Roman emperor to challenge all structures of oppression and promise new life to all those who have been put down and kept down by them.

2. Jesus' life as well as his teaching were highly subversive. He took a special interest in and identified himself with the poor and the sick, the marginal and the outcasts. He declared that the Reign of God belongs to the poor, rejoiced that the insignificant people, according to this world's standards, were the ones who understood what he was about and chose such people to be his disciples and form the basis for a new community of faith. Insisting on only one ethical commandment, that of *love* of God and neighbor, he shifted attention from rules and institutions to the quality of human life in

relationship; moreover, by his life as well as his words, he declared that true love moves downward; it is expressed in the giving of self to those who have no place and no worth.

One of the most amazing things about his life is that Jesus is always breaking out of the limits set by those around him, especially those set by dominant ideologies and structures. His concern is to see and move toward the richness of life available beyond them. Rarely, if ever, does he appear as the defender of existing institutions; time and again he challenges constituted authority, exposing its oppressive nature. His attention is focussed on the Reign of God, the new order that stands in radical opposition to the status quo. And he is confident that this Reign is already present in the world, that a vision and a power are already at work in history ordering all things in a new and more just way. Thus, the established order of injustice is not only under judgment but is being undermined, while the signs of a new age can be seen everywhere by those who have eyes to see.

3. It is this striking orientation toward the future rather than the past which constitutes the most revolutionary element in Jesus' teaching. The future utopia — God's Reign — is breaking into the present and thus must set the terms for life now. The end of history, which means its fulfillment, is imminent; thus all human life is set within the context of the ultimate life already begun. We can understand who we are only in the light of what we can become; the only social relationships that make sense or hold the promise of social stability and peace are those moving in the direction of God's Reign. And that Reign, as envisaged by Jesus, belongs to the poor and marginal; it is one in which those at the bottom are finding new possibilities of life.

Those who dare to look at the world as Jesus did will no longer hanker after an imaginary golden age in the distant past; they will rather yearn for and strive to build a new order more in line with this promise of life. Thus, the status quo loses its sacred aura; it stands under the judgment of a possible and more human future the coming of which it blocks. Change, with all the insecurity it may bring, loses its threat; life in the midst of change is set within the context of promise, the expectation of a fuller life.

Jesus went even further. He not only lived according to this new age but invited others to do the same and brought them together in a community. In the Sermon on the Mount (Matt. 5–7) he spelled out this ethic for his disciples, inviting them to live as if God's Reign were already here, sharing everything and turning the other cheek. It is thus not surprising that, with the coming of the Holy Spirit on the day of Pentecost, those who were converted sold their possessions and had everything in common (Acts 2:42–47; 4:32–35). The church was born as a community called to be a sign or the first fruits of this new age. Faithfulness to this vision called forth commitment to the transformation of society for the sake of those in need; a radically disjunctive eschatology became a way of life.

As a result of the first Exodus, Moses and the other founders of Israel gave their energies to the construction of a new society, with laws, institutions, etc. Jesus, confronting religious and social structures that had become sclerotic, challenged their foundations but did not propose alternative structures even to guarantee the continuation of the work of God. Rather, he was willing to give up his life, to choose the path of death, trusting in resurrection. He thus opened the way for an ongoing process of creation, in which those who would come after him might do ever greater things than he did. Resurrection is an act of *creatio ex nihilo,* the appearance of something completely unexpected, a quality of life that could not even be imagined on the basis of what went before. The Apostle Paul captured this when he spoke of the work of God, who gives life to the dead and *brings into being the things that are not.*

The radicality of Jesus' stance vis-à-vis the kingdoms of this world makes his influence highly subversive within established orders of oppression; it also provides the basis for a persistent critical ferment within any revolutionary process of social or national reconstruction. The vocation of every disciple of Jesus to love the neighbor, which is focussed on the poor and marginal, compels Christians to join in revolutionary struggles; this same vocation also compels them to challenge a revolutionary movement to be faithful to its declared goals. The fact that Jesus was killed by those in power and confronted their power with the power manifest in the weakness of the cross, challenges Christians to be especially sensitive to the abuses of power that so often lead to the betrayal of revolutions.

4. The writers of the New Testament are not primarily concerned about presenting a new ethical code. For them, Jesus is not a new Lawgiver, but the incarnation of God's concern for the

poor and marginal, a person who lives this concern and, in doing so, challenges the structures of power of his time. This leads to his crucifixion — and resurrection. The Gospels thus focus our attention on the *presence* of a unique person in the world. More than this, their witness to him is a witness of faith. They find that this person lays a divine claim upon them; in him God meets and addresses them. They sense an invasion of this world by another. As they respond to this person, they are offered life beyond the dead ends in which they are caught; they begin to perceive a new purpose for human existence in history and become participants in the creation of new possibilities of life.

Consequently, faith in Jesus Christ, the experience of being addressed by God in and through this person, brings with it faith in a radical renewal of history, the transformation of human nature, and with it, of the structures of society. Thus, St. Paul, as a consequence of his dramatic conversion, declares that he is united with Christ, which means a new world. The old order has gone, a new order has already begun (2 Cor. 5:13–17). And in the last book of the Bible, the Revelation of John, the author has a vision of "a new heaven and a new earth" (21:1) where Jesus Christ is enthroned. And he hears this Christ say: "Behold! I am making all things new" (21:5).

### The Pauline Witness: Die in Order to Live

The Apostle Paul is not usually considered to be a revolutionary; in fact, his thought is not often taken into account by Christians concerned about politics, except when Romans 13 is cited by conservatives claiming that Christians are obligated to submit to established authority. I believe that this reading of Paul, as well as the tendency to ignore him when struggling with the issue of revolutionary change, is most unfortunate. Those who settle for it deprive themselves of a rich resource for thought and action. Over the years I have found myself relying more and more on Paul to orient my life and witness in the world. As I do so, I discover that he not only pushes me toward a revolutionary stance but provides rich spiritual support for it.

The major reason for this is his conviction that Jesus Christ, through his death and resurrection, has initiated a new era in human history. With him a "new age" has begun. The "principalities and powers" of the world belong to the "old age" that is already passing away. In the light of these new developments, even the greatest achievements of the past, seen as the work of God, are of little importance: "Circumcision is nothing; uncircumcision is nothing; the only thing that counts is new creation" (Gal. 6:15, NEB). In this new age, no structure of oppression can stand; in it, "there is neither slave nor free, there is neither male nor female; for you are all one in Christ Jesus" (Gal. 3:28).

If we want to understand what Paul has to say about obedience to constituted authority, we need to keep this in mind. In his Epistle to the Romans, he is addressing new Christians who feel that their faith in Christ frees them to do anything; they need not take the structures of the world seriously. In writing to them, Paul stresses the importance of civil society and submission to that order. But what he has to say is far from being an endorsement of the status quo. Whatever purpose civil society may serve, the established order cannot lay a claim upon the Christian. Only love of neighbor can make such a claim upon us. "Leave no claim outstanding against you, except that of mutual love. He who loves his neighbor has satisfied every claim of the law" (13:8, translation by Paul Lehmann). This leads Karl Barth to affirm that "insofar as we love one another, we *cannot* wish to maintain the status quo. Instead, we do in love the next thing that casts down what has become old" (quoted in Lehmann 1975, 44).

But the most radical aspect of Paul's thought, and what he places at the very center of it, is his reflection on the meaning of Christ's death and resurrection for our life in the world and his insistence, based on his own personal experience, that it can and should serve as the pattern for authentic historical existence.

Long before his conversion, Paul had embraced the passionate hope of the people of Israel that God would replace the existing order with a new one. But the God who made this promise was bound to Israel for all time, the God of the Torah, considered to have existed even before the creation of the world. But Jesus detached God from the Law and declared that the new Reign that this God would establish would be given to people outside of Israel; it would be given to those who transgressed God's Law. For this, Jesus had been condemned by the highest authorities of Israel and crucified by Pontius Pilate. And yet, as Paul, offended by all this, engaged in persecution of Jesus' followers, he could not escape the possibility that God was present in their midst in a compelling way.

In this context, Paul's conversion could mean nothing less than the death of his previous way of life. He accepted it and found, on the other side of it, an experience of grace and of life he could not have imagined before. He experienced death and resurrection. As he lived this reality and reflected on the meaning of it, Christ's death *and resurrection* became, for him, the pattern for authentic human life. God had acted dramatically in the world in and through the death and resurrection of Jesus. This same God had led Paul to die to his past in order to receive life. Consequently, this can become the road to life for individual persons as well as societies. Individuals and nations are free to let go of their past, to die to it, and expect new and until then unimagined possibilities to open before them on the road to the future.

As Paul found in Christ the power to die to his past, he was also grasped by another dimension of Christ's death and resurrection. Those who dared to choose the path he had indicated were, by and large, the poor and powerless: "not many . . . wise according to worldly standards," nor powerful nor of noble birth (1 Cor. 1:26). This meant, for him, that the God who offers life to the world by this process has chosen the weak to shame the strong, and "things low and contemptible, mere nothings, to overthrow the existing order" (1:28, NEB). For this, they will pay a high price; they will participate, in some way, in the experience of death as Jesus did, but by doing so, they will become the bearers of new life for the world. As Paul put it, "we are . . . always carrying in the body the death of Jesus, so that the life of Jesus may also be manifested in our bodies" (2 Cor. 4:10).

In his study of the relation between the biblical story of the Exodus and modern revolutions, Michael Walzer declares:

> Since late medieval or early modern times, there has existed in the West a characteristic way of thinking about political change, a pattern that we commonly impose upon events, a story that we repeat to one another. The story has roughly this form: oppression, liberation, social contract, political struggle, new society (danger of restoration). We call the whole process *revolutionary*. . . . This isn't a story told every-

> where; it isn't a universal pattern; it belongs to the West, more particularly to Jews and Christians in the West, and its source, its original version, is the Exodus of Israel from Egypt. (Walzer 1985, 133)

I agree with Walzer on this; I would only add that the lines set by the story of the Exodus are not only followed but developed much further in the writings of the Hebrew prophets, the gospel narratives about Jesus of Nazareth, and the Pauline Epistles. Taken together, they suggest an approach to historical development and social change that even today strikes many of us as highly revolutionary. When these texts are read and studied in a faith community, they can contribute decisively to a profound spiritual experience that not only makes it possible for us to feel at home in times of revolutionary upheaval but may lead to dynamic participation in struggles for liberation and national reconstruction.

As I experience it, this faith stance nourished by the biblical heritage has a number of distinctive elements in it:

1. We experience a profound dissatisfaction with every established order of injustice. Sensitive to the sufferings of those at the bottom, we find intolerable any system in which a few enjoy great wealth and power at their expense. Living under the moral imperative to do justice, we find ourselves in opposition to all institutions and structures that institutionalize injustice. Captivated by a vision of a future world — a promised land, a Reign of God, the New Creation — we can never rest content with what our society or nation has achieved or feel completely at home in it. Rather, we find ourselves compelled to take a stand over against it, which brings us into conflict with the powers that be.

2. Faith in God leads us to expect to meet God in the midst of this conflict, intensifies our opposition to the status quo, and gives us confidence that this world can and will be changed. The God of the Exodus becomes known to the people of Israel as the leader of a slave rebellion; the prophets declare that to do justice to the poor is to know God; the New Testament hails Jesus of Nazareth, who takes upon himself the cause of the marginated people and is quickly killed by the highest religious and political authorities, as the incarnation of God. But this God leads the people of Israel to a promised land, assures them that their destruction as a nation

will be followed by a messianic age, and resurrects Jesus, whom the powerful thought they had gotten rid of forever, as the head of a new community striving toward the fulfillment of God's Reign promised to the poor.

3. This biblical perspective offers us an alternative to the destructive violence of unjust systems struggling to preserve themselves as well as to the social upheavals necessary to overcome them. In the light of this redemptive history, established orders of injustice are moving toward death. They are running down and are on the way out; the new order offering life to those at the bottom is already taking shape. In such a world, it makes sense for those who benefit from the status quo to let go of what they have, die to their former life, as Paul put it, and be surprised by resurrection. In this way, sclerosis and death can be overcome, those who most yearn for life and justice can use their energies for building a society offering a new future to all, and the achievements of previous generations can become a resource for the creation of a new world.

4. When those in power do everything possible to resist the mounting pressures for justice and block the way to the future, we will find ourselves called to be on the front lines of the struggle to overcome the resistance. Our reading of the Bible leads us to see that such structures produce death, that the longer they continue the more destructive they become. It prepares us to face the need for discontinuity — a decisive break with the past — at certain times, and assures us that order and stability will be found on the other side of change, as society is reorganized around the needs and interests of the people. And we will realize that if the order to be overthrown represents gross injustice and exploitation, the new economic and political order being constructed will stand in sharp contrast to it. Our vision of God's Reign and our confidence that social upheavals can open possibilities for moving closer to its realization should prepare us for and sustain us in the arduous struggle to create a more just society.

5. This same vision also compels us to take a critical stance toward the process of revolution and reconstruction at the same time that we participate in it. The new society, even with the dynamic participation of Christians and others passionately committed to justice for the poor, will not be perfect. The utopia of God's Reign stands in judgment on it. The only ultimate claim laid upon us is that of love to neighbor; thus our ultimate concern will always be

that of what is happening to people, especially those at the bottom or on the margin. And a vital faith, nurtured on the Bible, will focus our attention on dimensions of human life and relations often overlooked in the political arena.

# Chapter 8

# EXPLORING NEW OPTIONS
# IN A REVOLUTIONARY WORLD

OVER THE LAST THREE DECADES I have found that the biblical
perspective I have just outlined and the faith stance that goes with
it have gradually transformed my perception of what is happening
in a revolutionary world as well as my understanding of the role of
the United States in the midst of such upheavals. It has freed me
from fear of revolutionary change, forced me to look more honestly
at what is really happening in Third World struggles, and, most
important of all, made me aware of options available to the United
States that I had not considered earlier. In this chapter, I want
to present six such options that I believe biblically oriented people
can perceive and work for, options that, if explored seriously by
our policy makers, could open a new era in our relations with the
people of Asia, Africa, and Latin America.

## Ending Support for Oppressive Regimes

First, we can insist that the U.S.A. stop supporting regimes which
sustain established orders of gross injustice, oppress the majority
of their citizens, and rely on violent repression to remain in power.
These regimes are the major cause of instability and violence in
the Third World and their perpetuation tends to make violent
revolutions inevitable. It is not in the U.S. interest to be identified
with them or support them.

Biblical faith frees us from bondage to any status quo that is
destructive of human life, sharpens our awareness of the suffering it

brings, and assures us that it has no future in a world subject to the pressures of a just God who is making all things new. Whether it be the Marcos regime in the Philippines, the rule of Pinochet in Chile, the government in the hands of the traditional fourteen families and the military in El Salvador, or any of the other oppressive rightist regimes, certain facts about how they operate should not be ignored:

- Their political and military power is used primarily to preserve their power and wealth and they will go to any length to do so.

- The established order is based on the exploitation of the vast majority, but little will be done by those in power to change this situation. They do not want and will not work for a more equitable distribution of wealth or sharing of political power with the people. The problem is systemic: structures of economic, political, and social organization which together function to preserve present inequities.

- The logic of this system is in itself destructive and death-producing, and thus can sustain itself only through reliance on repression and violence.

Under external pressures, these governments may hold elections, take some small steps toward land reform, or promise to improve their human rights record, but these initiatives are not likely to go very far because they have no support within the system. Elections are held under a climate of fear; fraud is relied upon when necessary; and even when civilians are elected, the military may still play a major role. If land reform is legislated under pressure from the U.S.A., as in El Salvador, very little is done to provide peasants with the resources necessary to make it succeed, and those who receive land may be victims of violence.

To be sure, not all repressive rightist regimes are the same. Some of them may have the potential to take some steps toward democratization or make reforms serving the interests of the poor majority. Thus, it is important for us to study carefully what is happening in each country and assess realistically the potential for change. That is something quite different from harboring illusions about them or convincing ourselves that somehow such "authoritarian" regimes are more open or less destructive of human life than leftist "totalitarian" ones. The hard reality is that they tend to create dead-end situations in which their leaders will have to resign, be removed, or be overthrown before any significant movement toward democracy or social justice can take place. Their continuation in power can only lead to more violence, social instability and demands for more radical transformation.

We now know what the Shah of Iran and Somoza in Nicaragua did to create intolerable conditions that led to violent upheavals and to their downfall. While we still don't know what is going to happen in Haiti after Duvalier or the Philippines after Marcos, we do know that they robbed their own people while allowing the economy to deteriorate, thus making the task of national reconstruction extremely difficult. Their rule blocked the development of democratic institutions, and they persecuted or forced into exile many local and national leaders who could have contributed most to the development of democratic processes. Even in countries like Argentina and Brazil, where the military have pulled back and made room for civilian governments, their mistaken economic policies, corruption, and failure to orient the economy toward meeting the needs of the poor majority have left these governments with an almost impossible burden and created conditions for increasing social unrest. If we are really concerned about social stability in the Third World, then the time has come for us to repudiate once and for all a policy that, more than anything else we do, contributes to social unrest and leads to incredible human suffering.

## Supporting Those Who Can Create Conditions for Future Stability

If biblical faith leads us to believe that peace and stability are possible only when a society is moving in the direction of justice, we will be especially interested in relating positively to movements and governments working toward this end. If this goal can be achieved only as the established order is overcome, we will realize that it is in our national interest to support rather than oppose revolutionary movements that offer the promise of meeting this challenge.

Unfortunately, most of us North Americans are quite "underdeveloped" in our perception of this fundamental reality, at a time when increasing numbers of Third World people simply take it for granted. They know that when a very small ruling class has control of a system of integrated economic, social, and political structures that together function to serve their narrow self-interest, the interests of the majority can be served only as land is made available to larger numbers, political power is shared with the wider community, and a major change occurs in the distribution of income. They also know that those who have built up such a system in order to give themselves enormous wealth and power at the expense of the people are not inclined to welcome or permit such changes. Consequently, a stable future and more just society can come about only through the efforts of those groups capable of envisioning and working for *systemic* change and willing to pay the price of that struggle.

When we as concerned North Americans become aware of this situation and look more closely at groups and movements committed to revolutionary struggle, we may be surprised by a number of developments now taking place that should be taken into account by those who make and carry out our policy:

1. The new popular movements of urban and rural poor, of which we have spoken in previous chapters, represent a new force capable of laying the foundation for nonviolent change and the development of new democratic institutions in many countries. Their new sense of self-worth, their experience of shared responsibility in small grassroots organizations, and their willingness to risk death for their cause, make them an increasingly powerful force to be reckoned with. Their distrust of political parties and leaders and their experience of mutual empowerment in their own movements mean that they cannot be easily manipulated or controlled either by rightist regimes or in revolutionary societies. In Latin America, and to some extent elsewhere, the worldview out of which they operate is religious rather than Marxist; even when they draw on Marxism for analysis of society they seldom make use of the complex reasoning of dialectical materialism; their "Marxism" is blended with nationalism and elements drawn from their cultural and religious heritage.

To the extent that they have a chance to express their will politically, they offer an alternative to violent revolutionary upheavals. When they are blocked, repressed, and eliminated by the thousands as is happening in El Salvador and Guatemala, that possibility is destroyed while desperation increases and these people find themselves facing no alternative to violence. If we as a nation are interested in social stability and democracy in the Third World, nothing is more important for us than to understand and learn from, relate to, and support these movements.

2. Closer contact with the more traditional movements and parties on the Left will reveal that they represent a much greater diversity of background and ideology, and are more open to developing positive relations with the U.S.A., than we have thus far realized.

There are, of course, some movements that are ideologically rigid and irrationally violent, apparently so locked into their own illusory world of thought that they lose touch with the social reality they are hoping to transform. Such groups, however, are no more representative of the leftist forces in the Third World than fundamentalist groups are representative of contemporary Christianity. In almost all the Third World social struggles with which I have had any contact, I have found a rather wide variety of ideologies and strategies for change represented. And I have frequently observed that the growth of irrational fringe groups is directly proportionate to the desperation of the most marginal people, who find themselves totally excluded from national life and have no hope that their situation can be changed either through the normal political processes or in response to pressures from popular movements.

I know of no better example of this than what has been happening in recent years in Peru. There, *El Sendero Luminoso,* the Shining Path, has attracted a great deal of attention because of its ideological rigidity, its brutality, and its use of terrorist violence in Lima and elsewhere. All that is true, but when we denounce it, we would do well to remember several things: This movement has arisen and has its base among the indigenous population of Peru, people who have been victims of brutal exploitation and the most destructive marginalization for more than four centuries. It gains strength as the economic situation of the country deteriorates and the poor majority suffers greater deprivation. And most important of all, the Shining Path is a relatively small fringe group in the context of the forces on the Left in Peru at the present time. Among them, there are many who are products of the recent Christian concern for social justice, others who come out of a long indigenous Marxist tradition associated with José María Mariátegui, and a number of other groups representing a variety of radical ideological positions. Their efforts thus far have been hindered by their many divisions as well as their apparent inability to work out an effective political strategy. But in my contacts with them, I have been impressed by the fact that most of those I met were involved because of their concern for the suffering of the poor; they were working at developing viable economic and political alternatives to the present order and were willing to pay the price of a long-term struggle for change.

Just before his death in the mountains of Bolivia, Ernesto "Che" Guevara wrote a letter to his children, in which he said that "the vocation of every revolutionary is to love." Many of those involved in Third World struggles for liberation may wander far from this ideal. But, with these words, Guevara highlighted a fundamental element in liberation movements that is the source of their strength and the reason why they will continue to play an important role among people struggling for justice. If a significant number of these groups enter into a creative relationship with the new popular movements of which we have spoken, contributing to them at the same time that they allow themselves to be transformed by them, this will open new possibilities for the future of Third World struggles.

3. When we expose ourselves to the suffering of the people and realize that they will slip deeper and deeper into poverty and chaos until fundamental structural changes take place, we will recognize that the fate of the poor may well depend on movements capable of creating a new economic and political order. We will also realize that this is something that cannot be done by the tired old men willing to resort to repression and violence for the sole purpose of keeping what they have. Only those who suffer injustice because of their solidarity with the exploited are capable of carrying out such a formidable task.

This, I believe, is the reason why many North Americans who travel to Central America react so negatively toward what the U.S. is now doing and come to appreciate what is happening in Nicaragua. H. Craig Lewis, a member of the Pennsylvania State Senate, spoke for many I have known in his report on a trip to Honduras and Nicaragua published in the *Philadelphia Inquirer* on February 2, 1987. As someone who had never traveled in the Third World before, he mentions that his "most compelling emotional reaction was to the poverty — it is everywhere and all-consuming." But he goes on to say: "There is a totally different spirit and attitude between the Hondurans and the Nicaraguans. The Hondurans seemed to have little sense of self-determination. They seemed to have no solutions, no ideas for improving conditions, no enthusiasm and little hope. One derived the impression that they were convinced that only more U.S. financial support could make things better."

"The Nicaraguans, on the other hand, were upbeat in their outlook, albeit that they have an obviously difficult plight." "The breadth of ability among Nicaraguan leaders was impressive. They are well-educated, bright and articulate, pragmatic young people with a keen sense of history and a clear determination to change the squalid conditions under which their people live." "It was clear in discussions with both private citizens and government officials that there is a positive feeling with respect to the progress being made in education, health care and agrarian reform."

4. When we as a nation become aware of the contribution Third World revolutions can make to economic development and social stability, we may be surprised to discover that those who come to power through them are more inclined to have positive relations with us than we have thus far imagined. Triumphant liberation movements are not likely to be favorably inclined toward the U.S.A., especially if we have collaborated with the previous government in efforts to destroy them. And they will call for an end to certain forms of foreign domination that our nation has taken for granted for a long time.

At the same time, there are a number of factors that can contribute to a new quality of relationship, that can go beyond anything we have known until the present. When we demonstrate that we honor and support their efforts to overcome poverty and give the poor majority an opportunity to participate in national life, they may discover unsuspected connections between what we as a people have stood for over the years and what they are now struggling for.

We will be able to see that their priorities in using their resources are for economic development rather than military buildups. If the U.S.A. is not involved militarily in overt or covert efforts to overthrow them, they may be quite willing to engage in discussion and negotiation with us about our fears regarding their involvement in support of Third World liberation struggles or their possible inclination to turn to the Soviet Union for military support. If the U.S.A. is willing to explore new patterns of economic relations, we may find that these regimes are much more interested in developing stronger economic ties with us than with Soviet bloc countries and that they are also open to U.S. capital investment. In fact, when well established, such governments may offer much greater social stability and thus less risk for foreign capital than repressive military regimes.

## Perceiving and Supporting Alternatives to Violent Upheavals

Biblical faith assures us that the destructive violence of social conflict does not have to take place. It can be avoided — if only those who maintain structures of injustice that can no longer be tolerated are able to read the handwriting on the wall, recognize the necessity and inevitability of change in the direction of justice, and make room for it.

As we pointed out in the last chapter, the Hebrew prophets, Jesus of Nazareth, and St. Paul declare that structures of injustice set in process a movement toward death. But with equal emphasis they insist that individuals and nations can recognize the evil of their ways, let go of the structures in which they are caught as they die to their past, and participate in the creation of a better life for themselves and others.

At the heart of biblical faith is the conviction that human life can be renewed as women and men die to their old habits, get out of old ruts, and leave their dead selves behind in order to move into a new and richer future. The same applies to institutions, societies, and nations. The future does not open before us automatically; it is opened by our own inward death and renewal. Dead ends become the occasion for new beginnings. God becomes known to us in this process of renewal as the power that sets us free from our often desperate grasping for security and gives us new life on the other side of each death experience.

Some of us have had a taste of this in our personal lives, when we have dared to look critically at dead-end situations, or give up the security of well-trodden paths and face incoherence — only to discover that new options sooner or later opened before us. We may have experienced this in a variety of human relationships, which have been renewed and enriched as we have risked calling into question patterns of relationship which were no longer life-giving. And in the world of thought, we now know that many of the major breakthroughs in science have come through the efforts of courageous persons who perceived the limitations of accepted theories and were willing to abandon them and live with uncertainty while they engaged in the search for new ones.

The same principle applies to institutions. A dramatic example of this is the renewal taking place today in the Catholic church in Latin America, a renewal especially evident in Brazil. Traditionally, this institution played a major role within the structures of domination in each country, identified with and ministering to those at the top. It had a rigid hierarchical organization, which oppressed those within it, was largely cut off from the poor masses, and preserved relatively sterile liturgical forms and systems of thought. To many the Catholic church appeared to be locked into an inevitable process of decline.

And then, a few decades ago, groups of priests, nuns, and lay persons in many places began not only to look critically at all this but also to break with it by changing sides and identifying with the poor in their suffering and struggles. As their efforts continued and they gained, in a number of instances, the support of their respective bishops, many new and unexpected developments began to take place: the theology of liberation, the emergence and growth of the Christian base communities, the creation of new liturgies, and the increasing involvement of Christians in movements for change and liberation of the poor.

All this has, of course, led to conflict within the church but thus far it has contributed to the renewal of the religious institution from within, in striking contrast to what occurred in Western Europe in the sixteenth century. At that time, efforts at radical renewal were blocked, leading to religious schism and bloody wars, as a consequence of which each side in the conflict was deprived for several centuries of the resources of which the other community was the bearer. The struggle within the church is not yet over, but at the present time this dynamic movement provides a striking example of how change and renewal can take place within major institutions.

Unfortunately, what we so often see in Third World countries —

and in U.S. policy toward them — is the opposite of this: the failure to read the handwriting on the wall and bring about changes in time. As a result, social discontent builds up until violent explosions occur, and our nation spends its energies trying to seal the lids on pressure cookers.

Nowhere is this more evident than in Central America. As we pointed out earlier, when a democratic government attempted to bring about moderate reforms in Guatemala in 1954, the U.S.A. intervened to overthrow it, thus setting the stage for the repressive and violent developments that have taken place there since that time. In El Salvador, we continue to support a small ruling elite who are incapable of responding to the just demands of the majority and thus can stay in power only by relying on brutal repression as public protest mounts. We stood by the Somozas in Nicaragua while they created such a desperate situation for the people that it exploded in a popular insurrection. And now our government is supporting the *contras,* led militarily by the very people whose brutality and lack of concern for the interests of the people produced this insurrection.

Even with all this, it is not too late for us to change our ways and give support to those whose efforts to work for major reforms can still make possible a much less violent transition in the direction of authentic democratic societies based on social justice. In recent decades, many of the more progressive movements have been weakened or destroyed in one country after another. But, as we indicated above, a new instrument for social renewal and transformation is now being forged in the popular movements springing up in Third World countries.

Because of their potential to represent a large majority of citizens, their vitality, and the type of grassroots participation they encourage, these movements represent a force for *nonviolent* change, the likes of which has never existed before. In them, new democratic structures are developing through which those at the bottom can play a major role in shaping society and determining their future. And as small local groups come together to work cooperatively toward meeting their own material needs, they are laying the foundation for a new economic order oriented around local self-reliance. Our sympathetic understanding of and support for them could make an important contribution to the future stability and peace of the Third World.

## Supporting Efforts to Constitute a New Order

Oriented by biblical faith, we will be prepared to recognize and sympathize with the formidable task facing every successful revolution, that of *constituting a new order;* we will also be able to encourage those who shape our foreign policy to take advantage of the opportunities we have as a nation to contribute to the success of such efforts.

Every revolution has as its goal the creation of new and more just economic, social, and political structures. It thus represents a rare moment in the life of a nation, when the work of national regeneration can take a major leap forward. It is also an overwhelming responsibility for which no revolutionary movement can be well prepared.

Those of us accustomed to function within well-established patterns may find it hard even to imagine what is required to create new structures: to prepare a new Constitution, develop a new electoral system, or reorganize the economy in order to have a more equitable participation in economic life or in the distribution of goods. Yet every successful revolution must undertake these and other tasks more or less at the same time, learning by trial and error; its leaders must be willing to learn from the experiences of others while at the same time re-creating whatever they appropriate in their own unique situation.

In addition, successful revolutionaries take over a nation in an acute state of social disorganization, whose economic resources have been depleted during the struggle, and whose treasury may well have been robbed by those previously in power.

Moreover, a military victory does not necessarily mean the end of violent opposition. Some of those formerly in positions of power and privilege will leave the country but do everything possible to gain support abroad for their opposition to the revolution; others will remain but take every opportunity to sabotage efforts at national reconstruction. And since in poor countries there is not enough wealth to go around without major changes in its distribution, the greater the concentration of wealth and power in the hands of a few before the revolution, the more radical will be the measures taken afterward.

A new order will call for major changes in the ownership of the means of production and the distribution of goods, new opportunities for the people formerly excluded from the political process to participate in the exercise of public power at all levels, and the transformation of major institutions — in the areas of health services, education, the use of the means of communication, etc. — so as to give a new place to the people and their needs.

Looking at what is called for in the constitution of a new order, the biblical perspective I have presented has led me to a number of conclusions:

1. We can expect a revolution to bring into existence a more just society but not a utopia. Those who make revolutions often demonstrate an extraordinary passion for justice and concern for victims of injustice that leads them to expend tremendous energies at the task of national reconstruction. But revolutionaries will also struggle for power; they may be corrupted by it or use it repressively. They will make mistakes and will frequently fail to achieve their goals. The bureaucracies they establish may function slowly and inefficiently.

Facing this situation, biblical faith sensitizes us to the pervasiveness of human sinfulness and the way it corrupts all institutions including our own; it thus frees us from the temptation to expect perfection from those working for justice or to judge their failings more vigorously than we judge those of the sustainers of the status quo. We will not judge the Sandinistas in their treatment of the Miskitos by standards other than those we use to judge our own nation for its way of dealing with Native Americans or than those we use to judge what Brazil or Guatemala is doing today. Nor will we apply a standard to revolutionary regimes on matters of human rights violations, freedom of the press, or free elections different from that we use in judging others.

Moreover, our religious faith frees us from the need to expect salvation through politics. How frequently liberal persons who are disenchanted with life in the United States and see little hope for change in our society, tend to expect the latest Third World revolution to provide the utopia on which they pin their hopes for the future. When it fails to live up to their expectations, they feel personally betrayed and denounce it. When our hope for the future is focussed on the Reign of God which both points the direction for revolution and stands in judgment on it, we need not fall into this trap.

2. Those who look at the present in the light of the coming

Reign of God will realize that new economic and political structures arising out of revolutions today must be judged as to their value and effectiveness on terms quite different from those set by the previous order. In his study *The Structure of Scientific Revolutions,* Thomas Kuhn emphasizes the fact that a new scientific paradigm reorders the realm in which it operates and, for that very reason, can only be judged by new categories appropriate to it. The same applies to social revolutions.

In their attempts to bring order out of chaos and galvanize the energies of people around the construction of a new society, national leaders will mobilize large numbers of people in rallies and attempt to arouse great enthusiasm; they may make exaggerated claims for the revolution while denouncing its enemies. Such efforts may or may not contribute to eventual social stability but we will never be able to assess that if we judge them by criteria developed in times of greater stability. A new economic order based on the ownership of land primarily by peasants rather than large agribusinesses, and agricultural production oriented toward meeting the basic needs of the majority rather than export, will bring with it a whole new set of problems and possibilities for economic development. And the attempt to give people at the bottom new opportunities to take control of their lives and participate in the exercise of public power will focus attention on a range of issues quite different from those contemplated by those concerned only about "democratic" elections. Whether or not a revolution is moving toward its goals in each of these areas can only be determined by new criteria that are in line with a new vision.

3. Christians concerned about justice for the poor majority will realize that a new society meeting their basic needs will not be reconcilable with the old order. For the majority to have a decent life, those who formerly had great power and wealth will have to suffer loss. When, as in El Salvador today, the upper 2 percent of the population receive fifty times the per capita income of the lower half, some degree of economic democracy can be achieved only through the expropriation of some of their land and other means of production. When the vast majority of people in a country have been denied every opportunity to participate in the exercise of public power, national reconstruction will inevitably mean that those formerly in control will lose much of the power they once had.

Any such process of redistribution of power and wealth will involve social conflict and some degree of suffering for those who lose out; it may also involve some violence and lead to new injustices. The very complexity of the problem places a heavy responsibility not only on those most directly involved in revolutionary reconstruction but on us as a nation and a people. For we can act wisely in our relations with them only as we are free to understand and judge what is happening realistically and honestly, and in the light of the struggle for a more just social order.

Biblical faith forces us to ask ourselves why it is that we so quickly identify ourselves with those at the top who are losing out rather than the majority who have for decades if not centuries lost out and now have a new chance. Or why we react negatively to the polarization that occurs when the poor clamor for justice but not when the wealthy and powerful defend their position. When we consider the human cost of expropriation of land and restrictions placed on profits and incomes in Nicaragua, for example, we will also consider that in a few years more than 50,000 families who lacked secure tenure and access to sufficient land have now received titles to land and that steps have been taken to make basic foodstuffs, health care, and education available to those formerly living in extreme poverty. We will not calculate the human cost of national reconstruction without taking into account the human cost of maintaining an unjust status quo. Nor will we overlook the human cost of the consolidation of our own Western industrial revolution, as those who were formerly on top were displaced, families uprooted, or workers employed for long hours in factories under conditions we now consider inhuman.

4. Christian sensitivity to the transformation of human life in history will be able to appreciate and affirm the contributions made by revolutions even when they fall far short of their stated goals. Each authentic social revolution demonstrates to the world that a new step forward can be taken. It thus creates a new situation, opens the door to a new era, and thus helps to undermine an intolerable status quo, even when it fails to live up to its promise in its country of origin.

As North Americans, we will be able to deal creatively with the challenge of revolutions in the Third World only when we grasp this fact. The Cuban revolution has demonstrated, for all of Latin America and the Caribbean, that the economic resources of a small

Third World nation can be so used as to meet the needs of the majority and improve their lot, by providing them with food, health care, housing, and education. The Nicaraguan revolution has become a symbol of a new type of participatory democracy, in which the people at the bottom have a place of importance. It also has established the fact that social revolutions in the Third World do not have to be bound by rigid ideologies, regiment the people, or establish repressive structures, and that Marxists, Christians, and others can interact with each other and work together toward the building of a new society. Either of these revolutions can betray its original vision, or be destroyed by foreign intervention. But what they have demonstrated as possible cannot be blotted out and will inspire new efforts for years to come, which may well go beyond what they achieve.

### Facing the Challenge of Marxism from a Revolutionary Perspective

Biblical faith challenges us to look at Marxism and the role it plays in Third World liberation struggles *from a revolutionary perspective.* If we pay attention to what the Bible has to say about the transformation of the world, we will be as concerned as any Marxist about breaking out of bondage to sclerotic and death-producing structures and recognize how important it is, for institutions and nations, to start over again from time to time with a new rhythm and a new faith. And whatever the rewards we receive from the world as it is, faith in the God of the Bible awakens in us a deep concern for the poor, a passion for justice, and a yearning for a new society in which they will have a chance for a full life. Consequently, a profound spiritual transformation along these lines will situate us in the forefront of the struggle for justice at home and abroad; it will also transform our attitude toward Marxism as well as toward revolutionary regimes influenced by it in a number of ways:

1. Because of this experience of faith, we will be committed to working for social change as a necessary step toward justice. This frees us from bondage to the *fear of change* and allows us to see to what extent that fear is exploited by those who are trying desperately to maintain their wealth and power. No longer afraid of change, we are free to look at what is happening around us realisti-

cally, assess honestly what Marxism represents both positively and negatively in revolutionary struggles, and do everything we can to expose any form of anticommunism that poisons our national life by exploiting this fear of change.

No longer bound by fear, we will be able to perceive what rightist authoritarian governments are really doing, the crimes they are committing against their own people, and their inability to bring about reforms or lay the foundation for a stable society. We will realize that fundamental structural change must come about in many Third World countries and that the hope for it is to be found largely in liberation movements. And we will face the fact that in those countries where the poor majority suffer the greatest deprivation and exploitation, the required change involves a new economic order.

Once we arrive at this point, we will understand why it is that many Third World people who have the same concerns for justice and human well-being that we have are inclined to use Marxist categories of social analysis and come to the conclusion that some type of socialism will offer the best possibility for economic development serving the people. We will make a greater effort to listen to them and enter into their world of thought. When I have done this in recent years, I have frequently been taken by surprise. My inclination as a North American is to assume that those who are influenced by Marxism start out from a rigid philosophy of dialectical materialism that they want to impose on reality and on the world. But many of those I get to know don't fit this stereotype at all. Rather, they are primarily concerned about concrete goals that I also consider to be important: an end to the institutionalized violence of which so many poor people are the victims; economic development aimed at providing food, housing, and work for the large numbers of poor people at the bottom; an end to discrimination against marginalized people: peasants and urban poor, women, indigenous people; political processes involving larger numbers of women and men in the ongoing life of local communities and in national reconstruction and the affirmation of national dignity.

2. My religious faith leads me to affirm these same things and to do everything possible to work for a policy oriented toward their achievement. The fact that people working for them in one country or another are Marxists raises a problem with which I must

deal, but it cannot be a sufficient reason for me or my country to be opposed to these goals or to those groups honestly striving for them. When I do that, I go against the strongest imperatives of my faith; when my government does it, it works against economic justice and participatory democracy and alienates not only Marxists but many others for whom these are life and death issues. But, do we have an alternative? I'm convinced that we do.

The U.S.A. can take a firm stand in support of these goals and, by doing so, challenge the revolutionaries, whatever the extent of their influence by Marxism, to live up to their own ideals. The primary issue should not be that of ideology — whether or not they are, in some theoretical sense, "Marxist" or "Socialist" — but of practice — whether the society they are building really improves the life of the majority of its citizens, gives them a new place of worth and a major role in the decision-making process at all levels. Following this road, we will be able to encourage and support those who reject dogmatic loyalty to rigid ideologies in favor of a more humanist vision and an instrumental approach to Marxism and to ideology in general. And we will stand firmly on the side of those working for a restructuring of power from the bottom up over against bureaucratic and technocratic structures of a Leninist type.

The day we adopt such a policy, we may find that Third World revolutionaries do not have to be our enemies or work against our national interests. As Richard Feinberg and Kenneth Oye put it, "Basic U.S. interests are often threatened more by the customary American response to revolutionary regimes than by the revolutionary regimes themselves" (Feinberg and Oye 1983, 201). When we as a nation take a stand for economic well-being and democracy in terms that make sense to the people of the Third World and lead to social stability, we are carving out a new space for ourselves as a nation. Then, and only then, will we be in a position to challenge Marxists and other revolutionaries who fail to live up to their goals.

3. When we lose our fear of revolutionary change and dare to take a strong stand in support of the struggle of Third World peoples, we will be in a better position than we now are to assess realistically and respond to the threat of Soviet influence in Latin America and elsewhere. We will see that most revolutionary movements today are not interested in being under the domina-

tion of any superpower. In fact, the present U.S. policy that sees every struggle in the light of the East-West confrontation has been developed and implemented at the very time when Third World countries are moving in a quite different direction.

In the last few years a number of foreign policy experts have perceived something of which I have been aware as a result of my own contacts with university students and political leaders: a strong reaction on their part against the culture, structures, and power of both "East" and "West" and a sense that "capitalist" and "socialist" regimes have largely failed to bring either liberation or dignity to vast numbers of people. With recent developments in transnationalization of economic production and circulation, the revolution in the means of communication, and the emergence of many small nations on the international scene, a new space has been created for communities and nations to demand respect for their rights.

As people in social movements give more attention to their own history, culture, and conditions of life, they have little desire to fit into alienating systems of thought or of social organization imported from abroad. As Richard Barnet has remarked, "For most people in the world neither the writings of Marx and Lenin, the virtues and deficiencies of the Soviet central planning system, nor the betrayed dreams of a classless society are the issues that define reality" (Barnet 1981, 92).

The fact that a revolutionary regime calls itself socialist or Marxist does not necessarily mean that it will be pro-Soviet nor that Russia will be eager to embrace it. Countries in this situation want economic aid, which represents a financial drain the Soviet Union is unwilling to accept. And their leaders, if not threatened by U.S. efforts to destabilize them, will not be inclined to submit to Soviet control. In Barnet's words, "Every nationalist regime of the Left that has come to power in the Western Hemisphere has preferred to do business with the United States and to receive aid from the United States rather than relate to the Soviet Union — for obvious reasons" (p. 115).

Our present policy not only makes it impossible for us to make the most of the opportunities open to us for creative relationships with Third World nations; it tends to push those working for revolutionary change into the hands of the Soviet Union, even against their will. A change of policy on our part might reverse this trend;

it could also remove unnecessary sources of tension in our relations with Russia and challenge the Soviet Union to be more responsive to new nations and their people.

## Examining the Tendency of Revolutions to Betray Their Cause

Many of us assume that all revolutions inevitably betray what they were fought for; we thus justify acceptance of an unjust status quo and even collaboration with attempts to overthrow them. A biblically oriented approach to revolution can provide us with resources for more serious reflection on this problem.

I know of no philosophical or theological reason for concluding that revolutions have a built-in logic that leads them inevitably to betray what they stand for. As any other visionary social movement, they will fall short of their goals for a variety of reasons. Sooner or later, human self-centeredness, greed, and the corruption of power will manifest themselves just as they do in other societies. The impatience of those passionately dedicated to the cause of justice may lead them not only to consolidate power but to use it ruthlessly to establish a new order. As time goes on, some of the fervor and utopian vision of the first generation will be lost. The more intense the passion of the revolutionaries for overcoming the suffering of the poor, the greater will be their frustration as they perceive a widening gap between the society they envisioned and the order taking shape as the result of their efforts. Doctrinaire Marxists and others tend to be bound by blueprints of what should happen, will be inclined to try to force reality to fit their models, and may end up acting ruthlessly. And movements strongly influenced by Leninism will not be inclined to work for the restructuring of power from the bottom up in order to move toward authentic participatory democracy.

All this does not mean, however, that every Third World revolution is destined to betray what it stands for. As North Americans, we don't think that way about the American Revolution or the Civil War. If we look at what has been happening in Yugoslavia and China, we can see that even Communist revolutions of a more doctrinaire type have evolved in response to problems and new challenges they have faced. And the Sandinista Revolution in Nicaragua represents a new type of Third World revolution with a strong Christian element, following its own unique process of development.

Moreover, there are a number of factors at work today in liberation struggles that offer the potential for a more positive outcome. The strength of popular movements and their participation in the revolutionary process from early on represent a major challenge to traditional Leninist types of political organization. When those overthrown by a revolution are an extremely small minority while those who benefit from it represent the vast majority, national reconstruction has the possibility of being less violent and less repressive than it has been in Western countries. The fact that many of the new revolutionary leaders are more committed to the poor and their struggle than to a rigid ideology and are inclined to be pragmatic in their approach to social problems is something of no small consequence.

Of greater importance, in Latin America, the Philippines, and elsewhere, dynamic participation of Christians is destined to affect the outcome of revolutions from this point onward. Until recently, Christians were not present in these struggles except when a few isolated individuals became involved. After the triumph of a revolution, the majority remained aloof from the process, while those who became involved realized that they had not been a part of the earlier struggle and were thus hardly in a position to take a critical stance.

Today, Christian involvement in the process from the beginning means that their presence makes a difference in the struggle and gives them the right to take a critical stance. Those with a vital faith in a God who is active in yet transcends the political struggle will oppose attempts to make an idol of the revolution or absolutize a new order. Disciples of Jesus Christ live their lives in relation to a humanizing presence in the world that keeps their struggle focussed on the needs of people and undercuts obsession with the exercise of power as an end in itself. And those who participate in a revolutionary struggle from a base in a community of faith draw on resources provided by it to sustain their vision in difficult times.

In this regard, the Christian base communities and other expressions of the church of the poor represent a new factor that can have a strong influence on the revolutionary process as thousands of the poorest women and men are transformed into self-confident persons, sustained by their study of the Bible and a revitalized religious faith. In El Salvador, for example, they have given new strength to grassroots movements, and their willingness to die for their cause helps to mold a formidable force that the most brutal military and paramilitary forces find it difficult to contain. In Nicaragua, on the other hand, their continued presence in efforts at national reconstruction not only brings an important contribution to it but makes it difficult for those at the top to turn their back on the Sandinista emphasis on empowerment of those at the bottom.

Given these diverse elements, I believe that the time has come for the U.S.A. to do what it can to help Third World revolutions succeed and be faithful to their goals. Their success, with our encouragement, would create new conditions not only for international peace but also for us to play a more constructive role in the future.

# Chapter 9

# THE IDOLS OF THE POWERFUL
# AND THE GOD OF THE POWERLESS

AS BIBLICALLY ORIENTED PEOPLE become more involved in efforts to understand and affect U.S. policy toward Third World countries, they are frequently shocked by the type of opposition they meet in official circles.

For many, the federal trial of those working with the Sanctuary movement, held in Tucson, Arizona, in 1986, was something of a turning point in this regard. The judge in charge insisted that the issue at stake was that of respect for the legal system, and then proceeded to demonstrate that the legal system can be used to keep the truth from coming out, to serve political ends, and to get convictions. Those who were charged with serious crimes were not allowed to present their full case; they could not show why they believed that the government rather than the defendants was acting illegally, discuss what was happening in Central America or to the refugees they had aided, or tell the jury about their religious and ethical motivation.

Through their contacts with refugees, members of the Sanctuary churches have become aware of the suffering of the poor in Guatemala and El Salvador under brutally oppressive regimes, the devastation and death wrought, especially on the poor, by the war we support in El Salvador or through the actions of the *contras* in Nicaragua. But when Christians who know this try to engage in dialogue with government officials about it or raise questions about what our nation is doing to the masses of poor people in the region, they are often shocked to discover a callous lack of concern about such matters or find themselves attacked for providing "sanctuary to terrorists."

As North Americans we have been shaped by a liberal democratic tradition that assumes that we live in a reasonable world, among people who function rationally in positions of power. When we face crucial issues in our national life, we expect to find a climate of freedom in which to explore and debate them. We expect that leaders in a democratic society will encourage this process as the best way by which citizens can get to know what is really happening, make informed decisions, express their will politically and have it taken into account.

It thus comes as quite a shock to many when they discover that this cherished essence of our democratic way of life is not being respected, and that there is less and less space for open public debate. The more informed they become about what is happening in Central America, the more aware they are of the ideological distortion that is going on: brutal agents of death acclaimed as "freedom fighters"; those who live by repression, violence, and the maintenance of an order depriving millions of a chance for life heralded as defenders of democracy, while those attempting to open new possibilities, economically and politically, for the poor majority are accused of the worst crimes against humanity. In the place of public debate and the search for solutions to difficult problems, they see constant manipulation of the media and the use of all sorts of political weapons to win support for policies not in accord with the will of the people.

Much that goes on in the political arena, especially in this area of foreign policy, often has a strange "religious" aura around it. Policies are presented as dogmas not to be questioned and are defended with a spirit of intransigence reminiscent of religious fundamentalism. Theological language is much in use, frequently to attack those who oppose present policies. God is called on to give divine sanction to what our nation is doing, while those conceived of as enemies are denounced as belonging to a Kingdom of Evil. In this context, a narrow view of national self-interest is portrayed as the Ultimate Good, while those who question it can be branded not only as unpatriotic but as enemies of God. And those who defend the poor as well as many of the poor themselves find that the struggle against them has taken on a "spiritual" dimension.

At the same time, Christians facing this situation are finding that the Bible offers a fascinating interpretation of why this is happening. It not only lays before us the moral imperative to do justice as the one supreme ethical norm for individuals, communities, and nations; it claims that this imperative to do justice comes to us from beyond ourselves. In it, we are met by God; more than this, this absolute imperative is God; in the outcry of the neighbor in need, God addresses us unconditionally. In fact, this God who is Justice is presented to us as the creator of the universe, active in history to raise up the poor and set free the oppressed, the God whose determination to establish justice on the earth constitutes the future toward which history is moving.

From this perspective, the call to struggle for justice is a *divine* command; the struggle of the people at the bottom for a chance to have a full human life is the central dynamic of history, and the emerging aspirations of the marginal and oppressed are a major force moving the world toward what it can become, toward God's Reign.

In such a world, those who want to increase their wealth and power at the expense of others by maintaining structures of injustice face a very difficult, and ultimately impossible, task. They cannot escape this moral imperative of divine origin and they live in a world in which this presence inspires those on the bottom to struggle for liberation and sustains a dynamic movement of history which undermines the foundations of their established order. In such a situation, how can they hope to maintain their position, convince themselves of the rightness of what they are doing, or win the support of those around them?

The Bible has an answer, expressed in one word: *idolatry,* a word that means little to many of us today, but is central to the thought of both the Old and New Testaments. The only way to meet the challenge of this God of Justice is to take the very things God's presence calls into question and make gods out of them, ascribing to them a sacred or divine quality, worshiping them and doing everything possible to get others to do the same. In this way, the order they have created is identified with an all-powerful and transcendent Good; it is something sacred, which dare not be questioned by ordinary people. This sacralizing of a social order standing under judgment can give it a great deal of power, in the short run at least. But according to the biblical writers, it also sets in motion forces that are destructive not only of society but of those who make and worship the idols. And all efforts made to pull it off are destined to fail.

The making and worship of idols first catches our attention in the Book of Exodus, when the Israelites are wandering in the desert soon after their liberation from slavery in Egypt; later on, it emerges as a central concern of the prophets. In the New Testament, both Jesus and Paul make references to it, but the most dramatic presentation of idol worship is found in the Book of Revelation, where the author is speaking to Christians facing the power of the Roman emperor. The issue is thus dealt with at many different points in time, and in widely different circumstances. But, as Chilean theologian Pablo Richard has pointed out, "the majority of the biblical references to idolatry are found in a context of resistance to a struggle against oppression" (Richard et al. 1983, 4). Here we can only undertake a brief examination of some of these references.

### Mammon

In the New Testament this worship of idols is associated especially with *money,* or more specifically, the greedy pursuit of wealth. Best known are the words of Jesus: "No one can serve two masters; for either he will hate the one and love the other, or he will be devoted to the one and despise the other. You cannot serve God and mammon" (Matt. 6:24). Mammon denotes the personification of the greedy pursuit of riches as a god; the Greek word translated as "serve" really means "to be a slave of." For those greedy for material gain, money takes the place of God. Life revolves around its acquisition; as the ultimate value, anything necessary in its pursuit is justified.

In a number of places in his letters, St. Paul associates greed with idolatry but goes even further than Jesus in the denunciation of its pursuit. In a number of references to idolatry and its evils, Paul focuses especially on sexual immorality and "greed of gain" or "covetousness," using a word that literally means "wanting more." Associated with it are jealousy and fits of rage, selfish ambition and envy, dissension and robbery. For Paul, idolatry implies submission to the power of money, as something that takes possession of men and women, and this becomes a destructive force in personal and social relations. It is so contrary to God's purpose for human life and the world that those who become its victims "have no place in the kingdom of God" (see 1 Cor. 6:10; Col. 3:5; Eph. 5:5).

## Power

The prophets associate idolatry with the rejection of the liberating God of the Exodus, the yearning for power and prestige, and the need to create idols to justify and sustain this drive for power. In an early stage of the history of Israel as a nation, the kings are the ones most tempted to move in this direction and thus to establish and encourage the worship of idols serving their ends. In this way they can win the support of the people for their goals that are diametrically opposed to the will of Yahweh: the acquisition of wealth rather than justice for the poor, the exercise of oppressive power rather than the liberation of people, and the building up of military might rather than the search for peace.

In a dramatic passage, the prophet Isaiah denounces this betrayal and points out its direct relation to idolatry:

> Their land is filled with silver and gold,
> and there is no end to their treasures;
> their land is filled with horses,
> and there is no end to their chariots.
> Their land is filled with idols;
> they bow down to the work of their hands. (Isa. 2:7–8)

However powerful they may seem, Isaiah declares that such idols are after all only human creations and thus have no future over against the will of Yahweh. For "Yahweh alone will be exalted," while "the pride of men will be brought low" and "the idols shall utterly pass away" (Isa. 2:17–18).

At a later stage in their history, when the Israelites face captivity in Babylon, where they are once again sorely oppressed, the prophetic witness against idolatry takes on new dimensions. The rulers of Babylon are the ones who now make idols, idols that give them greater power over the Israelites and serve to validate this power. For this reason, they make a determined effort to get the people of Israel to worship their gods, and thus submit willingly to their power.

For Jeremiah (chapter 10) and Deutero-Isaiah (chapters 40 to

55), faith in Yahweh puts them in the most direct confrontation with all this. The same God who liberated the people of Israel from slavery in Egypt — and punished them when they departed from their historical vocation rising out of this experience — will now lead them through a new Exodus. They can look forward expectantly to a new liberation that only Yahweh can accomplish. Thus the idols of Babylon must be exposed for what they are: the supreme enemy of this divine project. For these idols have been made by human hands and thus are inferior even to human beings: "They have mouths but do not speak; they have ears but do not hear, noses but do not smell" (Ps. 115:4). They are like "scarecrows in a cucumber field" (Jer. 10:5). Whereas God carries, lifts and liberates the people, idols have to be carried around by those who worship them, as "burdens on weary beasts" (Isa. 46:1). The person who makes an idol out of wood falls down and worships it, pleading with it, "deliver me, for thou art my god" (Isa. 44:17). Those who worship Yahweh are transformed into God's image; those who make and trust idols grow to be like them (Ps. 115:8).

Nowhere is this contrast expressed more dramatically than in "The Letter of Jeremiah," found in the Book of Baruch. There the author declares that idols "will never save any man from death, never rescue the weak from the strong. They cannot restore the blind man's sight or give relief to the needy. They do not pity the widow or befriend the orphan" (Baruch 4:36–38).

## The Beast

In the Book of Revelation, the early Christian community, made up largely of poor and marginal people, faces the oppressive political power of the Roman empire. Here, once again, this power is related to idolatry. The empire is a new Babylon and imperial authority is described as a "beast"; those in power have no human feelings or qualities left in them. Yet the subjects of the beast make an idol of it, which serves to augment and legitimize its power. Together beast and idol work great signs and succeed in deceiving vast numbers of people, who worship the beast as they declare, "who is like the beast, and who can fight against it?" And such is their power that everyone must be branded, so that no one can buy or sell without this mark; in other words, they are excluded from society and condemned to death (chapter 13). Roman emperors thought of themselves as gods; Domitian demanded that he be addressed as "My Lord and my God," and anyone who denied him this homage had no right to live.

The Christians, on the other hand, declared their faith in Jesus as the Messiah of Yahweh and the only Lord. This person, who had taken upon himself the cause of the poor and powerless and for that reason had been condemned to death by the powerful, is not only alive but is engaged in making "all things new" (21:5). If this Jesus is Lord, then the struggle for justice over against the wealthy and powerful is at the center of history; Caesar's reign is coming to an end, for the lowly and destitute are destined to reign on earth. In the words of John, the author of Revelation, the scroll containing God's plan for the world, the clue to understanding the future, is sealed. No emperor is capable of opening it and discovering its secrets; only the Lamb, the humble and powerless Jesus of Nazareth, can do that.

To the Israelites living in bondage in Babylon and tempted to trust in the idols of Babylon for their liberation, Deutero-Isaiah declares that Yahweh and only Yahweh can lead a new Exodus from oppression. Likewise, John calls on his people to look forward to a day when the rulers of "Babylon," who claim to be gods, will be beset by seven plagues and God's people will cross over the sea in which their pursuers will be drowned like the pharaoh and his armies. Thus, the whole attempt to ascribe a sacred or supernatural character to the Roman empire is undercut; imperial power is subverted, and this idolatry is exposed for what it is, a futile attempt to block God's work of liberation by ascribing divinity to those who are determined to continue to dominate and oppress.

## The Golden Calf

The story of the golden calf in Exodus 32 deserves special mention. In it, the Israelites make and worship an idol not of a powerful political leader or of a foreign god but of *their own God* who delivered them from slavery in Egypt.

The people of Israel have escaped from Egypt, but they are having a hard time in the desert. They are headed for the promised land but will be able to create a new society beyond the oppression they left behind only if they undergo a radical transformation and submit to a strenuous discipline. This is what God has called them to be and do and Moses is leading them in this endeavor.

But many of the people are weary. The task before them is overwhelming and they have lost hope. When Moses leaves them for a time, they reject his leadership and what he represents; they call on Aaron to make an idol of their God and willingly turn over to him their gold rings to be used for that purpose. When the golden calf is made, they hold a great celebration and worship it.

According to Pablo Richard, all this shows that the Israelites do not want to abandon the God who brought them out of Egypt but to make an image of this God so that they can be in control and bring an end to the pressures under which they are living (Richard et al. 1983). Instead of facing daily a divine call to build a new world, they want a God who will console them and even allow them to return to Egypt.

Yahweh and Moses react immediately and violently to what has happened. This act on the part of the Israelites represents nothing short of the betrayal of the transcendent God who wills the creation of a new world of well-being and justice — *in the name of this God*. It is thus the ultimate and most dangerous expression of idolatry.

When political leaders fall into idolatry, the stage is set for a direct confrontation between those in power and persons of faith. For biblical faith provides a foundation from which to expose what is going on as well as the spiritual resources necessary for such a struggle. In a concluding chapter, we will attempt to speak more specifically about what this means in relation to U.S. foreign policy.

## Chapter 10

# EXPOSING AND OVERCOMING IDOLATRY

IN RECENT DECADES, theologians and political scientists have called attention to the modern tendency to deify the nation-state and have conceived of it as a consequence of the erosion of religious faith in a post-Christian era. If people no longer have a vital faith in God, it is easy for those in power to give ultimate value to the state and win support for it among men and women who are groping for a spiritual anchor in times of personal and social crisis. Those who make this claim, however, often overlook one important historical fact that in the Western world, the sacralization of the nation-state has occurred at a time when structures of domination and exploitation serving a relatively small elite have been challenged from below by large segments of the population.

Nearly a half century ago, a distinguished political scientist, Carl Friedrich, pointed out that "the exaltation of the absolute value of the state" is a "reaction in Europe and America to the emergence of the democratic faith" (Friedrich 1942, 43). As this faith opens the way for increasing numbers of people from the middle and lower classes to claim the right to participate in the exercise of public power — and also to have a greater share of the benefits of society — those who have most to lose place more and more stress on *order*. Their "unexplained major premise" is that "order is more important than anything else, or, to put it in more modern terms, that security was more important than anything else" (p. 59). To meet this challenge, says Friedrich, this state must claim omnipotence, which is something traditionally associated with the deity.

137

From this point, it is only a short step to conceiving of the state as "the final and ultimate value, the earthly god to which all common men must be subordinated, yes, even sacrificed" (p. 48). Those in power are able to escape being considered oppressors by identifying themselves with God. And in the name of God, they are free to do anything.

We in the U.S.A. have not only ignored this development; we have assumed that while the deification of the state may unfortunately occur from time to time in other societies, it cannot happen here. When I studied with Reinhold Niebuhr in the 1950s, I was quite convinced by his analysis of how this had happened in Hitler's Germany and Stalin's Russia as well as his argument about the inevitability of idolatrous elevation of the state in Marxist societies. I also found convincing his claim that the U.S.A. was different, because we have built the foundation for an open, democratic society in which such absolutization of unjust structures of domination cannot easily occur.

However, when I look around me today, I realize that the situation has changed. To an astonishing degree, the very things we have denounced as demonic consequences of state idolatry are not only making their appearance here but seem to be gaining ground. Here I would like to call attention to several of them.

## The Sacralization of Our Values

The very values that Niebuhr saw as saving us from idolatry are now being transformed into idols. *Freedom* and *democracy* are affirmed as absolutes, objects of religious loyalty, and whatever we do in the name of these values has a sacred aura about it. The images or Freedom and Democracy have been abstracted from social reality and exalted to the point that we need only pin them as labels on our policy or on any government we support in order to block critical examination of what is being done in their name. Concern for these values is of such a nature that we need not concern ourselves with the suffering and death of vast numbers of poor people or of others who are struggling for justice. And such is the mystique surrounding Freedom and Democracy that, in their name, repression and support for regimes dedicated to destroying the foundations of democracy are justified.

Moreover, the National Security State becomes an end in itself.

Massive spending for defense and the militarization of society that accompanies such an all-out effort — here or in Central American countries — are of such exalted importance that they should not be questioned; to do so can be seen as near blasphemy. In such a climate, it is easy to ignore what is really happening to people, cultures, and societies under these policies, at home and abroad. The state does not exist so much for the welfare of the people, as people for the welfare of the state. And the checks placed upon the use of such power by ethical norms or international laws need not be honored.

Any nation with great power is inclined to consider itself more altruistic, its system more valuable to the world, and its motives purer than they really are. The U.S.A. is no exception. But in a democratic society, we can expect that such pretensions will be vigorously challenged, especially when they produce policies that fail to serve our national self-interest and work against human well-being elsewhere.

But what we see more and more in evidence today is a movement in another direction. When Third World nations are protesting against our unrestrained use of overwhelming power, our nation not only invades Grenada, bombs Libya, and carries on a massive military build-up and display of power in Central America, but extols these actions as contributing to the defense of freedom, the preservation of order, and the establishment of conditions for peace. When our economic exploitation of other countries is challenged, our nation is portrayed as the great benefactor of humanity and our type of economic development — along with our continued economic penetration — in Third World countries is heralded as destined to bring great benefits. And as the emergence of new nations calls for more complex patterns of international relations, the U.S.A. strives to put itself in a position from which it can be the final arbiter of the destiny of Latin American nations and attempt to bring an unruly world under its control.

The adoption and pursuit of such unrealistic policies by the most powerful nation in the world can represent a serious threat to international peace and stability. But that danger is augmented when such policies are so exalted that they take on a sacred character. Niebuhr time and again warned against any national ideology that claimed to be a "scheme of universal redemption," in which the interests of a nation were identified with "the ultimate purposes of God in history." This, I believe, is the danger we face at the present time.

When those who make and carry out our policy are bound by such an ideology they lose touch with reality and encourage those who report to them to ignore it. Making constant use of the noblest ideals detached from reality, they create an atmosphere in which they can give free reign to their lust for power and their desire to control the world. The recently exposed dealings of members of the National Security Council with Iran and the *contras* not only illustrates how this process works but also reveals how disastrous the consequences can be.

## The Demonization of Those Who Oppose Us

Those who worship idols live in a world threatened by Evil Demons as well; they create them, permeate society with their spirit, and live in fear of them. Over the last several years, the climate of fear produced by such idolatry has had a profound effect on U.S. policy toward Third World countries, especially in Central America.

As a consequence, the problems in Central or South America are not seen as due to poverty, exploitation, or the refusal of a few ruling families or groups to share power and offer the majority a larger share in the economy. Rather, the crisis is due to the unrest of the poor, the influence of those working for social change, and movements of national independence. All those involved in such things must be doctrinaire Marxists, serving the interests of the Soviet Union.

All problems disturbing a status quo presumed to be serving our interests must be due to another power, an Evil Empire against which the United States must struggle with all its might. The world is divided sharply into good guys and bad guys. The bad guys are not adversaries with whom we might be able to negotiate but enemies to be destroyed; they are devils who cannot be trusted and with whom we should in no way bargain.

Marxism in general and Soviet Communism in particular are the embodiment of this evil. The Soviet Union thus appears as a monolithic empire, obsessed with gaining more and more power until it takes over the world, with tentacles everywhere on earth. It has large numbers of agents everywhere, including the U.S.A., and North Americans who question the dominant ideology or policy are seen as serving its interests. Inherently evil, a "Communist" movement or regime can do nothing good, but any crime against humanity can justly be attributed to it. On several occasions, when I have spoken about the literacy campaign in Nicaragua, what I saw being done to develop farm cooperatives for peasants or the excitement of many poor people about their new opportunity to participate in public life, I was immediately told either that all these things were only ways of deceiving and winning the support of the people, or that I had been duped by the Sandinistas and was not presenting a true picture.

When this spirit takes over, those under its influence cannot grasp the social and political realities of Third World countries, understand the role of Marxism there, or perceive clearly the nature of the Soviet threat, wherever it may exist. If all international crises are, at the bottom, the product of this Evil Empire, then we need not face the real causes of poverty or social unrest or concern ourselves about the suffering of the people. We need not make an effort to understand whether those working for change are really Marxists, much less explore what is happening in Marxist ideologies and movements in one country or another. We need not contemplate the possibility that such movements and regimes might be willing to establish positive relations with the U.S.A. And we are under no compulsion to examine honestly what changes may be taking place in Soviet Communism or the role the Soviet Union is playing in Central America or elsewhere. In such a context, reason loses out. Nations seeking to follow a more independent line in relation to us have no chance to demonstrate their willingness to be good neighbors. If they do not appear to be on our side, they must be our enemy, and consequently they must be controlled by Moscow. If they are not so inclined, we can follow a policy that will compel them to depend more and more on the Soviet Union for survival and thus confirm our logic.

Under such conditions, critical examination of foreign policy is discouraged; journalists and scholars, actors and church leaders, soon realize that it is not to their advantage to take a stand in opposition. Those who dare to do so may find themselves looked upon not just as unpatriotic but as guilty of blasphemy. They are considered to be evil and almost anything done to harass or discredit them is justified. Latin Americans who oppose U.S. policy or Mothers of the Disappeared may be denied visas to this country. Christians in Latin America who support the struggle of the poor can be denounced as "Marxists" in efforts to discredit them. Sanctuary churches and offices of solidarity groups have been burglarized. And Colonel North, working out of the White House, can orchestrate vicious media campaigns to defeat members of Congress known to be critical of the administration's policy.

In its all-out struggle against Evil, our nation ends up falling victim to the very things it is struggling against: dependence upon a rigid ideology that blocks understanding and provides the foundation for irrational acts; restrictions placed on freedom and civil rights; reliance on force and intervention in the life of other nations, in defiance of international law. By our intervention in Third World countries and our support of regimes that are fundamentally antidemocratic, we negate the ideals for which we stand and thus destroy any basis we might otherwise have to challenge Communism. Having ourselves fallen victims to idolatry as a nation, we are in no position to challenge idolatry as it manifests itself in the Communist world.

### Reliance on Hypocrisy and Deception

The worship of idols produces hypocrisy and deception and those who deceive others end up deceiving themselves as well. When those who use imperial power for their own benefit portray what they are doing as the Supreme Good, and categorize those who have taken on the struggle of the poor for justice as the incarnation of Evil, they create a situation in which they can maintain their position only by reliance on falsehood and deception. Only thus can they bridge the gap they themselves have created between the ideals they proclaim and their actions. This is especially true in the U.S.A. when those in power appeal to our democratic tradition and to our belief that we use our wealth and power to support democratic societies serving the interests of the people.

In the last few years, the policies pursued by the Reagan administration have been so out of line with the ideals articulated that hypocrisy and deception have become the order of the day:

- The administration claims it is seeking to establish peace in Central America while relying almost entirely on military solutions. Thus, it talks of peace and speaks favorably about the Contadora process while sabotaging that same process. It claims it cannot accept any negotiations with the insurgent forces in El Salvador who are trying to "shoot their way into power" while going to any length to support the *contras* who are attempting to do the same thing in Nicaragua.

- It affirms a policy encouraging economic development serving the interests of the people and supporting reforms that would contribute to that end, while giving political and military support to regimes that maintain structures of extreme privilege and use repressive measures against individuals and groups struggling for change.

- The administration claims that it is supremely concerned about Soviet penetration in Latin America and elsewhere while refusing to examine seriously to what extent that danger exists and forcing nations that want to be more independent of any superpower to turn to the Soviet bloc for survival.

- It refuses to take a strong stand against the governments of South Africa or Chile, claiming it should not interfere in the affairs of sovereign states and emphasizing the value of "quiet diplomacy," while determined to overthrow the government of Nicaragua.

- The Reagan administration has portrayed itself as the great enemy of international terrorism even to the point of bombing Libya, at the same time that it has supplied arms to Iran and allowed the CIA to be involved in assassination plots and other terrorist activities and train the *contras* in the use of terrorist tactics.

In fact, in its dealings with Nicaragua, the administration has been engaged in a long history of deception and hypocrisy. It justified its support of the *contras* by accusing the Nicaraguan government of supplying arms to the insurgent forces in El Salvador. When the studies of a CIA investigator clearly proved this to be false, that policy was not changed. It condemned the Sandinistas for building up their military forces to defend themselves while the CIA was arming and training the *contras* to invade the country and overthrow them. It declared that the elections to be held in Nicaragua would be invalid because they did not have wide participation of opposition parties, while making every effort to convince opposition candidates not to take part and offering them money if they withdrew. The administration has attacked the Sandinistas for brutal treatment of the Miskito Indians but has ignored what is being done to the indigenous population in Guatemala or Brazil, or the degree to which attempts were being made to make use of the Miskitos to overthrow the Nicaraguan government. And when the Nicaraguan government began to negotiate with Brooklyn Rivera, one of the Miskito leaders, in an effort to find a solution to the problem, it appears that Colonel North arranged for money to be paid to Rivera in order to break off the negotiations.

In the short run, this policy may have succeeded in deceiving many people and thus winning their support. But, sooner or later such deception can only lead to a crisis of confidence at home and the loss of our credibility abroad. Informed citizens eventually conclude that they have been deceived and realize that they cannot trust their government; Third World people become even more sceptical — if not cynical — about what the government of the United States is doing. As Carlos Fuentes, the Mexican novelist, remarked: "Why is it that the United States is so impatient with four years of Sandinismo when it was so tolerant of forty-five years of Somocismo? Why is it so worried about free elections in Nicaragua but so indifferent to free elections in Chile? And why, if it respects democracy so much, did the United States not rush to the defense of the democratically elected president of Chile when he was overthrown by Pinochet?"

Perhaps most serious of all, those who live by deception of others may eventually come to believe the lies they use and assume that the U.S.A. is really doing what they claim. When this happens, those who make and carry out our foreign policy are so out of touch with reality that their actions not only have destructive consequences in Third World countries but work against our national self-interest as well. Idols created out of fear, to make a nation invulnerable and help it maintain its power, end up leading their makers astray. Having lost touch with reality, they imagine dangers that do not exist and engage in actions that produce greater social unrest and international instability.

## The Political Encouragement of Idol Worship

Those who worship idols demand that others do the same. When the state is sacralized and those in power expect its citizens to worship it, the normal political life of a democratic society is subverted. The political struggle is transformed into a religious struggle; national self-interest becomes the Supreme Good and policies defined as serving this end become articles of faith to be believed in rather than questioned. A good citizen is someone who is patriotic, which means giving unqualified support to established policy.

Under these conditions, the foreign policy of a nation takes on a religious aura, but this type of religiosity stands in the sharpest contrast to biblical faith. Authentic faith gives absolute allegiance to God alone. It calls for a thoroughgoing commitment to the poor and marginal in their struggle for justice, but neither God nor Justice can be identified with a specific political program or movement. Rather, faith in the God of the Bible frees those who believe from the compulsion to absolutize their perspectives, policies, and parties and compels them to look critically at all they are doing in the light of a transcendent vision.

Moreover, if God is on the side of the poor in their struggle for justice and history is the arena in which this struggle moves forward, then those who worship God will have a strong desire to analyze what is happening in society, especially in situations of conflict. For the closer they come to understanding economic and political realities and to finding adequate solutions to social and international problems, the better prepared they will be to serve God and neighbor. On the other hand, there are those who, in their attempt to assure their survival, sacralize structures threatened by pressures for justice coming from below; they will be tempted to close their eyes to what is happening around them. By transforming Freedom and Democracy into religious symbols, Noble Ideals to be defended at all cost, they need not engage in serious examination of what is being done in any specific country in the name of such ideals. Worship of idols thus blinds its followers to reality and rational discourse about foreign policy gives way to the emotional defense of dogmas. In fact, the most irrational positions, when sacralized, will be the ones that are defended most vigorously, for only in this way can faith be sustained in policies so out of line with reality.

This, I believe, provides us with a clue as to what has been happening in U.S. policy toward the Third World in recent years, especially in relation to Central America. The Reagan administration has discouraged serious public discussion of its policy. It has paid little attention to the best scholars in the field or to others with long years of experience living and working in those countries. Instead, it set up the Kissinger Commission or order to use public figures and scholars to provide a rationale for positions already taken. The administration has ignored the will of the American people and showed little respect for Congress, making use of every means possible to gain congressional support for its policies. Instead of engaging in dialogue with our Latin American neighbors about the problems of the region and possible solutions to them, the administration has concentrated its efforts on bringing each country into line and sabotaging their proposals for negotiations.

Dogmas are to be believed in, not questioned. Thus, the aim of the administration is to create a public climate in which critical examination of such dogmas is discouraged and the media of communication are constantly used to gain popular support for current policy. When the president announces a policy and course of action, the people should close ranks behind him. Anyone who questions the wisdom of his decision can be accused of being unpatriotic.

In our discussion of the biblical perspective on idolatry, we referred to the story of the golden calf in the Book of Exodus. The curious thing about this idol made by the Israelites was that it was an image, not of a pagan god but of Yahweh, their own God who had liberated them from slavery in Egypt. Discouraged with the cost of the long struggle for liberation, they yearned to return to the fleshpots of Egypt. So they made the Golden Calf, an image of Yahweh that *they could control* and use for their own ends.

In our Western world, especially in the U.S.A., where most popular religious symbols are of Christian origin, our worship of idols tends to be of this type. God, Christ, and verses from the Bible are constantly being used to justify and support policies that maintain our power and privilege in the world but ignore the suffering and work against the liberation of the vast majority of people in one country or another. The name of God is frequently invoked by public officials, appeals are made repeatedly to the religious sentiments of people, and the Bible is time and again quoted in defense of actions taken. When the stories first broke about what Colonel North had been doing in relation to Iran and Nicaragua, he told reporters to look at the "eighth Beatitude of Matthew 5," which reads: "Blessed are those who are persecuted for righteousness' sake, for theirs is the kingdom of heaven."

In this context, it is not surprising that the Reagan administration should seek to win the support of religious leaders who will pronounce God's blessing on their policies. Or that popular TV preachers should attract attention as ardent defenders of these policies when they are using Christian symbols to provide divine sanction for the longing of so many Americans for upward mobility, material well-being, and affluence — and all the while raising millions of dollars largely from poor and lower middle-class people to build their own empires and, in some cases, live in luxury.

Such idolatrous use of the name of God can only happen with the erosion of authentic biblical faith, as new revival movements revive less and less of the heritage of faith and place a "Christian" veneer on anything having to do with the established order and the American pursuit of wealth and power. How else can we understand the ease with which some evangelists seem to feel at home with those in the centers of power, pronounce God's blessing on what Jesus denounces as the service of Mammon, or identify U.S. policy in Central America with the will of God? How else can someone as pious as Colonel North dare to apply to himself a Beatitude that blesses, and offers a special place in the Reign of God, to those who are persecuted for the cause of *justice?*

Authentic worship of the God of the Bible brings with it a sense of confidence in the ultimate triumph of justice and thus creates a spirit of freedom and of openness, even toward one's enemies. The worship of idols tends in the opposite direction. Those who give ultimate value to the preservation of what they have must work much harder to sustain their faith and thus block out hard realities that challenge their position. After returning from a trip to El Salvador with a team investigating the human rights situation there, I was shocked to find that frequently persons with whom I spoke simply did not want to hear our report or hastened to tell us that we were not presenting a correct picture. When we urged them to listen to the witness of Salvadorans they were even less interested. And on a number of occasions, I realized that even when we presented the best documented report, those who did

not want to hear it ended up attacking us for presenting it.  I
then understood that there is only one step from this reaction to
attempts to harass those who are critical of present policy.

### Justification of Human Sacrifice

Idols give those who worship them the right to decide over the
life and death of people; they justify, and even demand, human
sacrifices.

In the context of faith in the God who wills justice on earth,
social and political structures have legitimacy only to the extent
that they serve human ends; their existence should be understood
in instrumental or functional terms.  Jesus expressed this most
emphatically when he declared to the Pharisees that the Sabbath
was made for the sake of human beings, not human beings for the
sake of the Sabbath (Mark 2:27).

But when the state and its policies are absolutized, an abstract
entity that cannot give life to people takes on an existence of its
own and becomes an end in itself.  When this occurs, concern for
what happens to women and men has secondary importance, if
it is taken into account at all.  And anything that gives a sacred
aura to structures legitimating the domination and exploitation of
the weak by the strong calls for human sacrifices.  Such structures
nourish themselves on death.

This, I believe, may give us a clue as to why those who make
our policy at the present time so rarely take into account how
our interventions affect the masses of people in Central America
and elsewhere: whether or not the people of Nicaragua want their
country controlled by the *contras* or what a *contra* victory might
mean for the poor majority there; what has been happening to the
people of El Salvador under the regime we have been supporting,
what the consequences of our military action are for these people,
or what life is really like for the peasants in those zones more or less
under the control of insurgent forces; or what our militarization of
Honduras is doing to those who live in that country.

Whenever ultimate value is given to an order serving the interests of the few who are rich and powerful, such idolatry inevitably
becomes antihuman and calls for major sacrifices.  Those who control the International Monetary Fund and other aid programs, as
well as many Third World leaders, constantly call for austerity

and sacrifice. As Delfin Neto said when he, as Brazil's minister of planning, defended the austerity measures adopted by President José Sarney, "there is no progress without sacrifice." But the interesting thing is that those who make such declarations do not volunteer to make sacrifices for the sake of progress or call on others in their position to do so. Rather, they *impose* such sacrifices on those least prepared to make them, the poor majority.

Thus, in recent years, our government has adopted policies that have made it possible for those who are wealthy to become wealthier, while cutting back on services that might provide housing for the poor, jobs for the unemployed or medical care for those deprived of it. In other words, our society has been able to continue to function, for the benefit of some, through human sacrifice. The same thing happens in many Third World countries that we support. Idolatry serves to legitimate and give free reign to insatiable appetites that devour people.

When an economic system, political movement or nation is sacralized, its enemies as well as anything else that hinders its progress are seen as evil. The elimination of such evils, which serves to "purify" society, can be conceived of as a service to God and can be carried out with righteous zeal. The poor, victims of an unjust economic system, are to blame for being in that position and can only be helped if the welfare system is discontinued and they are forced to take initiatives to improve their situation. We recognize the horror of what Hitler did to "purify" German society by eliminating the Jews, homosexuals, and others, or the work of death squads in Brazil or Argentina during the time of military rule as they "purged" their countries of thousands who were seen as defiling it because they were protesting against their poverty, challenging the legitimacy of the established order, or just happened to be seen as social "misfits." But how sensitive are we to efforts being made in our own country by groups attempting to "purify" it through zealous attacks on various groups of social misfits and especially on those who can be branded as "Communists" and then harassed and denied basic human rights?

Men and women who have survived torture in Latin America in recent years frequently speak of the fact that those who tortured them seemed to get a special satisfaction out of doing it. In other words, the act of torturing can have a certain "religious" quality about it. To offer a sacrifice means to take something human, transform it into something sacred through its destruction, and offer it up to a god as an oblation. And as the person making the sacrifice is seeking to gain salvation, the greater the sacrifice, the greater its "saving" power. When those being tortured are seen as the incarnation of Evil, the supreme threat to a sacred social order, the most brutal and violent treatment leading to mental derangement and death is not only justified; it is offered as a sacrifice on the altar of national security. Attempts to engage in rational moral discourse with those who engage in such rituals will prove as futile as with adherents of fanatical religious sects.

In sharp contrast to this, the God of the Bible makes human sacrifices unnecessary. This God does not demand of human beings more than they can give. God is at the center of a dynamic movement in history giving life to those deprived of it as more just structures are being created. To the extent that this happens, there will be no need of immolations or expiations. Jesus Christ, as the incarnation of this God, offers his life as a sacrifice on the cross, thus annulling the need for any other sacrifice. As the author of the Book of Hebrews put it, there is no further need for human sacrifice since Christ "did this once for all when he offered up himself" (7:27). Christ takes upon himself all the suffering caused by the injustices and oppressions of history and stands at the center of a community of faith whose members continue the struggle for justice. For them, the sacrifice of the poor and marginal is intolerable, but they know that they can combat it only as they follow the example of Christ.

## Communities of Faith Respond

To the extent that this tendency toward idolatry comes to play a significant role in our national life, especially in the shaping of policy toward the Third World, any serious attempt to change that policy becomes a formidable task. Open public discussion of issues will not be encouraged; appeals to reason will have little effect. Those in power have the media at their disposal and will not hesitate to make use of them to create and sustain the myths they desire; and when they sacralize our most cherished traditional values and exalt them as the goals of foreign policy, they may well gain wide popular support. Those who stand in opposition can easily be denounced as enemies and zealously attacked. And when policies that are so far out of line with historical reality fail to achieve what they promise, they can easily lead to frustration and poison the political atmosphere.

Political movements and parties are not usually prepared to respond to this challenge. In such situations, faith communities with a clear understanding of idolatry and how it functions have a unique opportunity. Among people trying desperately to go against the grain of history, those who believe in a God who works to establish justice are oriented toward the future and face demands for change with confidence and hope. They need not be afraid to face the reality of what the U.S.A. is doing abroad or of the struggle of dispossessed people to create new economic and political structures. The more those in power rely on lying and deceit, the more compelling will be Christ's mandate to know the truth, so that the truth can make us free (John 8:32). When their government puts its trust in military solutions, justifies brutal repression of popular movements, overlooks the work of death squads, and supports military ventures that indiscriminately kill civilians, people of faith dedicate their efforts to the empowerment of the powerless and respond to this violence against the poor by striving for greater solidarity with them in their struggle. And, as anyone who has been in close touch with this new breed of Christians from South Africa or Central America can perceive, those who choose this path often have a sense of life, a spirit of joyfulness and hopefulness, that stand in sharp contrast to the spirit of those trying to destroy them.

This response on the part of a community of faith to the idolatrous worship of the state evokes a violent reaction from those who rely upon it, precisely because it challenges them on their own ground and exposes their religious pretensions. For this reason, in many parts of Latin America in recent years, rightist military regimes have frequently shown special zeal in arresting, torturing and even killing Christians working for change, especially grassroots leaders in poor communities. If we are correct in what we have said about the temptation to idolatry in the U.S.A. today, we should not be surprised if government officials and agencies denounce, harass, and seek ways to prosecute Christians opposing their policies on theological grounds.

In this struggle the state making idolatrous claims for itself is at a serious disadvantage, in spite of all its power. For when

Christians are attacked for not giving ultimate allegiance to those in power, they respond by praying for them. This can become a highly subversive act because it expresses deep concern for them as persons and in their exercise of power, while declaring that their power is legitimate only when they are subject to and serve something beyond themselves and their class. When those committed to the poor and oppressed in their struggle for liberation are willing to die for their cause, the powerful are powerless to impose their will even by the use of violence and death. Their violence ultimately exposes the lies by which they live. And as Christians involved in this struggle have a new experience of the presence of God in their lives, the resurrection of Christ expresses their hope that the martyred representatives of the people will have the last word in history.

As men and women of faith are subject to this violence and draw on the resources of their religious heritage, they will be in a position to articulate a new vision of their nation and its role in shaping and supporting a new international order. They will understand that our future depends on changing sides and discovering how to relate to and support the struggles of the Third World rather than the small elites. They will realize that this can happen only as our own society is transformed in the direction of greater social justice. And they will also see that such transformations can come about only as the result of fundamental changes in the system of values of the American people.

But the transformation of our values is fundamentally a religious matter. It has to do with a sense of the meaning and purpose of life and the symbols by which we put our world together. Consequently, our concern for a new policy toward Third World countries leads us to recognize the important role religious communities are called upon to play at this point in time and how ill prepared most of them are for this task. For we are in no position to challenge our nation to be more concerned about oppressed people of the world until we have a new experience of the God of the oppressed and respond to the imperative laid upon us by the gospel to seek justice above all else. And we can challenge the religious pretensions of those in power only as our lives are grounded in a faith based on a deeper understanding of the Bible and sustained by prayer, spiritual disciplines, and renewed liturgical life. If these resources are not available to us in the church as it is, we will have no choice but to struggle for the formation of new communities of faith among those who share these commitments and are engaged in this search for spiritual grounding.

Those determined to preserve the status quo at any cost accuse progressive Christians of having reduced the gospel to a political agenda and of having lost concern for transcendence. But it may well be that this is not what they most fear. For what is now beginning to happen across the land is quite the opposite. A new concern for the suffering of the poor of the world and for what the U.S.A. is now doing to them has led many Christians to a new experience of spiritual renewal, a new life of faith. It is leading to the formation of small but vital new communities, in the Sanctuary movement and elsewhere, in which women and men are finding new depths of faith they have never known before. It is this reality that challenges most radically our present policies and provides motivation and orientation for long-term struggles for a new foreign policy. It represents one element in our national life that may make it possible for the United States to play a more positive role in the struggle for life for the emerging peoples of the world and for an international order offering peace with justice.

# WORKS CITED

Barnet, Richard J. *Real Security: Restoring American Power in a Dangerous Decade.* New York: Simon & Schuster, 1981.

Beker, J. Christiaan. *Paul the Apostle: The Triumph of God in Life and Thought.* Philadelphia: Fortress Press, 1980.

Crozier, Michael, Samuel Huntington, and Watanuki Joji. *The Crisis of Democracy.* New York: New York University Press, 1975.

Feinberg, Richard, and Kenneth Oye. "After the Fall: U.S. Policy toward Radical Regimes." *World Policy Journal,* Fall 1983.

Friedrich, Carl. *The New Belief in the Common Man.* Boston: Little, Brown and Company, 1942.

Galtung, Johan. *The True Worlds: A Transnational Perspective.* New York: The Free Press, 1980.

Gilder, George. *Wealth and Poverty.* New York: Basic Books, 1981.

Johansen, Robert C. *The National Interest and the Human Interest.* Princeton, N.J.: Princeton University Press, 1980.

Kohn, Hans. *American Nationalism.* New York: Macmillan, 1957.

Lehmann, Paul. *The Transfiguration of Politics.* New York: Harper & Row, 1975.

Moore, Barrington, Jr. *The Social Origins of Dictatorship and Democracy.* Boston: Beacon Press, 1967.

Richard, Pablo, et al. *The Idols of Death and the God of Life.* Maryknoll, N.Y.: Orbis Books, 1983.

Rosenstock-Huessy, Eugen. *Out of Revolution: Autobiography of Western Man.* New York: Four Wells, 1964.

von Rad, Gerhard. *Old Testament Theology.* vol. 2. *The Theology of Israel's Prophetic Traditions.* New York: Harper & Row, 1965.

Walzer, Michael. *Exodus and Revolution.* New York: Basic Books, 1985.